Wagging Tails, Swishing Tails, Fluffy Tails and Other Tales

By

Judy Fuson

ISBN: 1-4033-8265-4 (E-book)
ISBN: 1-4033-8266-2 (Paperback)

Library of Congress Control Number: 2002094944

This book is printed on acid free paper.

Printed in the United States of America
Bloomington, IN

1stBooks – rev. 04/09/03

DEDICATION

This book was written for all the animals, birds and living creatures that have passed through my life and for the ones I have yet to meet.

TABLE OF CONTENTS

FOREWORD

In the past few years my role has changed from that of a pet psychic and animal communicator to that of a teacher. At first, most people were content to have me read their pets; then a shift in energy started, and now my clients want me to teach them how to talk with their pets for themselves. Along with requests for workshops and lectures came the request for a book on "How do you talk to the animals?" Finally the time was right: here is my book on animal communication.

I want this to be more than a collection of animal stories. I want to offer my readers some new ideas and insights, but I do not want to dictate or imply that my way is the only way. I believe the best way to learn this language is in a group with pets, students and teachers. In this situation everyone shares the energy, both animals and humans. The energy comes to us in the form of telepathic thoughts, visual images and as feelings in our bodies. The language of the animals is not linear and it requires us to be flexible in our understanding of how animals talk and what they have to say. I have done my best to explain these concepts in some detail, but I must emphasize that it takes many hours of practice with your animal friends. This language takes time to learn, but anyone can do it if they stay open to the animals and believe that they can do it.

All of the animals, birds, fish, and insects have a purpose on the earth. They are here to help us grow spiritually and make us aware of how interconnected we are. We all coexist, but in learning this language we can open doors to new levels of communication and to new experiences with all these living beings.

ACKNOWLEDGEMENTS

This book would not have been written without the help of my friends in Tucson, Arizona, Sue Helm and Kaye Patchett. I also thank Linn Major and Susan Shurtleff, old friends who contributed their wonderful photographs for this book. Finally all my clients who pushed me to write this book, thank you.

CHAPTER 1

How I Became an Animal Communicator

I grew up as an only child, on a Thoroughbred horse farm in Lexington, Kentucky, with my pets as my best friends and playmates. At times I knew intuitively what my dogs or horses wanted but I could not explain how I talked to them without using words.

The dogs, horses, and cats all brought different experiences to me that increased my wish to learn to talk and communicate with them.

My earliest memories are of playing with my dogs and exploring our yard with my dog following me. My parents loved dogs, and they were a large part of my family life. My mother had pictures of me as a toddler with Skipper, a Collie who came to visit from the farm next door. It seems when Skipper's own human children grew up he moved next door and adopted me as his new job. My mother used to say that I learned to walk by pulling myself up on his long silky coat as he stood by me; then he walked beside me to steady my first steps. In looking back at photo albums I notice that he is in many photos of me, keeping a very watchful eye in my direction.

The first dog I have clear memories of is Molly, a Dalmatian. Molly loved her human family and knew her job was to protect us from outsiders. She would nip at my friends if they got too close to me and she would always position herself between my mother and any people she did not know when visitors came to our door. The family story of Molly reaching up and holding my mother's arm to prevent her from spanking me was told many times. She didn't bite, but my mother knew that Molly felt I didn't need such punishment for whatever I had done. I remember Molly sleeping on a chair in my room when I was sick and home from school. Mother would have to force her to take a bathroom break or make her leave the room to eat, and it would not be unusual for Molly to develop a sore throat if I had just had one.

My special companion from grade school through high school was Butterfly – a small, black dog of very mixed heritage. He came to me as a puppy, a gift from our farm employees, and received his name because I had been watching a beautiful group of butterflies on the day he was given to me. We became inseparable almost immediately. He slept on the foot of my bed, and followed me all over the house and farm like a four-legged shadow. If, in his opinion, I had stayed up too late over my homework, he would drag his blanket from the bed to wherever I was working and sit on it until I put both of us to bed. He adapted to childhood games of dress up and tolerated wearing hats, scarves and other pieces of clothing, many times posing for pictures in his finery.

In time horses joined my dogs as my best friends. The dogs had been my guardians, companions and friends, but my horses gradually became my teachers. I had grown up riding a large bay pony named Prince. My mother always supervised all my barn and horse activities, but I longed to spend time alone with him. As I grew older and more independent, the horses became my escape from everyday life. Not only could they run and jump, but in riding them I felt that I could fly away too. It was so easy to forget school or problems with my parents when I went to the barn. I just lost myself in caring for the horses and in riding. I had a large farm to ride over and could be anything from an Indian to a cowboy or a jockey. I knew my horses enjoyed carrying me around the farm. We had nothing to accomplish, we were just in the moment having fun.

As I got a little older, I began competing in horse shows. I had been taking riding lessons for several months and entered my first horse show only because my friends were doing it and I didn't want to be left out. At ten years of age I received my first ribbon, a second place, on King my lesson horse, and started a new world of horse shows and competition. I always loved challenges and was very competitive. I didn't feel I had to win but I always strove to be in the top three or four places in each class I entered. My competitive and perfectionist nature started to take a beating. The challenges of showing horses over jumps, jumping each fence and doing it all correctly grew as my abilities and levels of riding skills grew. My family was continually pushing me to new levels, which meant a new horse, a new trainer, and higher expectations from my family. Throughout all of this I bonded completely with each horse I rode. In the horse world there is a term called "over-mounted," meaning that the horse was more skilled, more educated and worked at a much higher level than his rider, and I was usually over-mounted. In an effort to raise my riding skills, professional trainers and riding lessons became a large part of my life. No matter how bruised I was from falling off or frustrated from not accomplishing my trainer's goals, I always stayed in tune with my horses. And I started to watch horse trainers, my own and those I met at horse shows, to see how they trained their horses.

Living on my parents' farm introduced me to the world of breeding and raising Thoroughbred horses. All the horses were raised to be racehorses and I was able to follow their progress from birth to the breaking and training that prepared them for the race track. Our lives revolved around the farm, and I loved to accompany my parents when they made their daily rounds. Every day the horses were examined for physical injuries, and there were regular meetings with the farm manager to talk about the health and training of each horse. I was also able to watch the farm veterinarians, blacksmiths and horse trainers while they worked at their respective jobs on the farm.

I soon observed that some of these men developed a closer and more understanding relationship with the horses. Others moved through their jobs quickly, and failed to establish a secure relationship with the horses. I watched the exercise riders and trainers work with the yearlings. It was easy to see which of them developed a trusting relationship with the young horses, and I started to realize that these riders knew intuitively what to do to give each horse confidence and guidance during their weeks of training. The people who the horses responded to most readily seemed to have a sixth sense that completely connected them to their horses.

In my opinion this intuitive part of working with horses was just as essential as learning training methods. Through all of my work

4

with horses the most important things that I learned were to be quiet, observe the animals and try to tune in to their thoughts and feelings by observing their body language. This taught me the main aspect of nonverbal communication that I stress today – be quiet, clear your mind and wait for the animal to send you a message.

Throughout high school and college, my horses and dogs remained the most important part of my life. In the years from grade school to high school, riding horses, either in the show ring or fox hunting with our local hunt club, occupied most of my time. I was fortunate that my parents supported my interests, purchased horses for me to ride and sent me to good instructors for riding lessons. Working with horses dominated my early life, and the fact that I later became a horse trainer was a natural progression of events.

CHAPTER 2

Early Lessons From My Horses

It was during my teenage years of meeting new trainers and reading about classical methods of horse training that I knew I would become a professional trainer. Now my goal shifted from competing to a new goal of actually training and getting to know my horses. I began to recognize that the thought in my head while riding was as important as what my legs and hands were doing. One horse I rode would always shy and buck in an area about three feet from the entrance to the riding ring. When I realized where he bucked each day, I knew that I was anticipating his behavior when he reached that place in the ring. In effect, I was sending him a message to buck before we ever reached that spot.

My horses started to teach me how to ride them and how to control my mind when I was on them. I realized that random thoughts had no place in my head during a riding lesson or training sessions. One of my coaches believed that talking to your horse during a lesson was very helpful for both horse and rider. He didn't care what we said, but he emphasized using a quiet, steady tone of voice. He was on the right track. Talking quietly and calmly kept the rider's mind focused, and kept up a mental and physical connection with the horse during training sessions. This same trainer encouraged lots of pats on the neck and rubbing our hands on the horses' necks to keep them quiet. Now I know that the hand contact was a great way to transmit positive energy from the rider to the horse.

Out Late, a chestnut gelding that I rode during high school, became a show and pleasure horse for me. While I was in school Out Late boarded at a training barn so I could take riding lessons and ride with my friends. We would trail ride throughout the countryside around the barn where I boarded him. During one of those rides, he provided me with one vividly memorable experience.

One spring afternoon we were ending our ride by taking a trail that crossed in front of a farm house. As I passed the house, I saw a large, fawn-colored Great Dane standing on the steps of the house. The trail was several feet from the house and yard, and was used regularly by other riders. His barking increased as I passed the house, and continued as I left the woods and entered an open field by the main road. Before I knew what had happened, he was out of his yard and chasing my horse. I urged Out Late to a trot, hoping that the dog would stop. Knowing that running encourages a dog to give chase, I continued at a slow trot. Then the dog ran to my right side and lunged at me, grabbing the calf of my leg and trying to pull me off my horse. Frantically, I tried to shake him off. He let go, ran to the front of my horse and leapt for his throat. Out Late reared up, and I fell off backwards. The dog chased him for several feet, then turned back toward me, growling. I was in the middle of an open field, with no way to escape. When Out Late saw the dog turn back, he ran to me, put his head down, and chased the dog out of the field, saving me from a very serious attack. When he returned to me, I saw deep

7

lacerations from bites on his throat and neck. I remounted and jumped Out Late over the fence surrounding the field, not wanting to take time to open the gate. When I got back to the barn, I discovered that the dog's teeth had torn through my tall leather riding boots, my jeans and my knee socks, leaving me with a bruise on my leg but no real bite. Out Late required several weeks of veterinary care, but was not seriously injured. The Great Dane's owner had him euthanized shortly after the attack.

When this happened I had not started animal communication and so I was not able to ask the horse if he knew a reason for this attack. The owner of the dog did tell me that the dog had chased other trail riders, but had stopped before any horses were hurt. Out Late's action in rescuing me convinced me of the links and bonds that can be established between animals and their humans. My horse was safe from the dog, yet he returned to save me. I had not sent him mental images to return to me. The only thought I had was that I was completely defenseless against the dog and Out Late returned as my rescuer.

The year after college I started to train Bold Paddy, the horse that became my best friend and taught me the most about communicating with my horses. My father gave Paddy's mother to me when I was in high school. She was a very kind Thoroughbred mare, originally purchased for her potential as a brood mare. She had failed, several years in a row, to conceive a foal and my father eventually gave her to me to train and ride. I never lost hope that she could produce a foal and I planned the mating with a stallion on my parents' farm, knowing intuitively that the resulting foal would be the perfect horse for me to show. I was with our foaling attendant when Paddy was born. When he was delivered he looked up at me and whinnied, saying, "It's me, don't you remember me?" Over the next twenty years I came to realize that we truly did know each other and that he had entered my life in order to open doors that would take me to a higher level of understanding and awareness. I believe his purpose was to show me that he and I were part of one Universe and one Universal Plan.

As Paddy grew up I spent every minute I could with him, brushing him, playing with him and working on his socialization with humans. When he stopped growing he was 17 hands and 3 inches. At that time he was one of the largest Thoroughbreds in the show ring. He was a perfect size for me. Large horses attracted attention at a show and I needed a tall horse because I was over six feet tall.

When Paddy was a year old he was broken to ride with the rest of my father's yearlings. After his early lessons, he was turned out to grow and develop his body before I started training him to be a hunter for the show ring. I was fortunate enough to take him to a wonderful training barn and start his work under the guidance of the barn owner. I now became the only person to ride him, and at first I assumed that our close connection came from the hours we spent together as he grew up. Then I noticed that I could get him to trot or walk by thinking the command – without making any body movements, such as moving my legs, changing the length of my reins or by using my voice. All I had to do was think it and it happened. Watching my friends ride and seeing other trainers at horse shows, I perceived that some of them did not know why their horses behaved in certain ways and had no intuitive understanding of what their horses liked or disliked. At the time I did not realize that I had established a special connection with Paddy that let us work and train on a higher level than other horse and rider combinations. In the next year we started showing in the hunter rings, winning and attracting attention wherever we went.

Paddy was a very large, dark chestnut, energetic horse and loved showing his playful side at horse shows. No matter how often he pranced and played I always knew that he was just having fun and he expected me to be tolerant of his behavior. We had a great understanding and I allowed the rambunctious behavior in return for near perfect rounds over the jump courses. When he entered the ring to start a course he became focused and intent on doing the best job he could. Paddy always gave me a feeling of great confidence. I sensed that he was telling me that he would never physically hurt me, that he knew I could ride him over each jump and that he knew when to play and knew when to focus on his job as a show horse. I never questioned our relationship or how he could read me and I could read him – it just happened and I accepted it as a normal part of our life together.

My success in showing Paddy led me to a career as a professional show horse trainer. I started my own business in Lexington on my father's farm, giving riding lessons, training other people's horses and working toward my goal of being a successful rider and trainer.

Paddy stayed with me, eventually going into retirement and living with me until he crossed into spirit at the age of twenty-eight. He was always very possessive of me and would let me know how much he resented the fact that I rode other horses. Whenever he saw me ride another horse, he would rear and whinny loudly to attract attention and make sure that I knew how unhappy I was making him. Paddy always wanted to be the one special horse in my life and he kept that special place all the years he lived with me. He continues to keep it now that he is in spirit and assists me as a spirit guide in the work that I do now as an animal communicator.

As part of my spiritual growth and in search of answers about events in my present life I did a series of past life regressions. As I focused on my past lives with the help of my spirit guides, I hoped that discovering certain events in my past lives would give me new insight on events in my present lifetime. I discovered Paddy in many past lives, always as a horse that I worked with. In each regression I could sense how much he cared about me and how much he has always wanted to help and protect me. I know now that one of his gifts to me, in this lifetime, was the recognition of spiritual connection between humans and animals.

Working with Paddy made me aware of the highest levels of understanding and communication between horse and human. He allowed me to expand my thinking and to realize that many other animals could communicate with people in the same way. To receive his thoughts I only had to keep my mind open and wait for a thought or feeling to come to me. I just knew and felt what he wanted me to know. Our years together taught me to be open to the thoughts of all the animals, not just horses, and motivated me to go on with my work in animal communication.

CHAPTER 3

My Introduction to Animal Communication

My success with Paddy brought clients and students to my new horse training venture, which was just building and beginning to grow when my father died. His death was unexpected and caused enormous changes in my life. As well as my own business, I now had the management of an eight hundred acre horse and cattle farm, complete with my father's horses and his clients. I was totally unprepared to manage a Thoroughbred farm. All my previous experience had been in the area of riding and showing horses.

Three days after my father's death our professional farm manager left for another job – then our two employees left, and I became responsible for the care of sixty horses and the hiring of new employees. Our farm population included horses of all ages and it became my job to oversee the breeding and foaling of mares, raising the foals, preparing young horses for commercial horse sales, breaking yearlings for the racetrack, working with racehorses and handling the farm stallions.

I was blessed that the Universe sent me two excellent teachers who could advise me on all aspects of Thoroughbred care, as well as helping me develop my interpersonal skills to deal with the farm's clients. One of these men was my veterinarian. The other was a horse trainer from the racetrack, who truly became my mentor in the ways of horses and people. Both showed me different ways to work with horses, observe their habits and learn from the horses by watching, waiting, and staying open to the animals' thoughts.

The other life-changing event that occurred in my first years as a farm manager was seeing Beatrice Lydecker, an animal communicator from California, on a local television show. Here was a woman who could not only talk with animals, but could actually receive their replies to specific questions, and explain in detail how this new language worked. I bought her book, *What the Animals Tell Me,* and tried to teach myself to ask questions of the animals and get their answers. I loved the book but felt that I was a failure at learning this type of communication. Bea explained how the pictures that form in our minds and the animals' minds become a visual method of speaking. She stressed one of the most important aspects of nonverbal communication: that there is no picture or image available to represent a negative word. She explained that we often emphasize negative behavior by the words we use to give our pets commands. The principal idea was to put all words and commands in the positive and thus picture the dog doing a positive behavior. For example, saying, "Spot, don't jump on the bed" actually sends a picture of Spot jumping on the bed, because there are no pictures for a negative word. Instead, use a positive command: "Spot, sit on your dog bed" – or the floor, or wherever you want your dog to sit or lie down. However, in spite of all my efforts to master this new form of communication, I was not able to confirm that I had sent a picture to ask a question nor did I feel that I was getting any type of response back from the animal.

I went back to using my intuitive feelings as a way of working with the horses, but I really wanted to ask the new horses that came to board on my farm personal questions: who their horse friends were, what people they liked, what they liked to eat, did they enjoy being racehorses, and so on. I still felt that I would never understand their responses, or even know if they had bothered to try and talk back to me.

Fortunately for me, Bea returned to our area for more television shows and announced that she would be giving a workshop in animal communication in the area where I lived. This class included a lecture and a practice session where students talked with pets who accompanied their owners to the practice group.

The practice session showed me how images fly instantaneously from the animals to us. I learned that animals see things at their own eye level; and that they actually do see a fairly wide range of color. The only image I received all day was from a dog who had been hit by a car – he showed us exactly what it was like to look back over his shoulder and see what looked to me like part of a tire and a fender coming toward him. When it was my cat Watchkitty's turn to meet the group she was fairly silent. She sent pictures of a red plastic bowl that was her food dish, but had very little to say about her family at home. When asked if there were other pets at home she only showed pictures of our two dogs – completely ignoring the fact that she also shared the house with another cat. Bea explained that this was a normal response and that it implied that she wanted to be an only cat. I asked the group to ask her about her experience in climbing trees – again there was no response from Watchkitty. Then I told the class the story of coming home to find her "stuck" in a tree. After much coaxing, she started to slide backward down the tree trunk. As she inched her way down, her claws reached a place with no tree bark – at this point she let go of the tree and fell about twenty feet, landing on a stack of plywood. She looked like a flying squirrel as she fell, hit the plywood and bounced in the air. Then she had walked off as if nothing had happened. In my mind this had to be the most traumatic event, as well as the most memorable, in her short life. At the class she never mentioned this adventure, even when asked specifically about it. Bea explained that something we perceive as a huge event does not necessarily produce the same reaction in our pet. After years of my own work with pets I know now that my cat was giving me an example of living in the moment. She was not physically hurt or emotionally damaged by her fall – why should she dwell on it? She continued to climb trees until her death, and always showed me, by what I considered her reckless behavior, that she truly lived in the moment.

I went home to practice on the new horses that clients sent to my farm – but I still felt like a failure in animal communication. In the next few years I took more of Bea's workshops and, by listening to their responses to various questions, learned how animals view the world. As I got to know Bea better I discovered that she did more than talk to pets. She could look at a photograph of a pet and do a reading from the picture. She could communicate from long distances without seeing or knowing the pet, and she also did body scanning – checking for any physical problems as well as telling you how many puppies were in your pregnant dog and what color they would be. I was fascinated. Now my new goal was not just to talk with dogs or horses standing next to me, but to reach a level of skill like Bea's.

In those first years of learning animal communication I tried to involve as many of my friends as possible in my new world. As we learned together it became obvious that our pets could direct different thoughts to each person; and that our own pets often talked more openly with their owner's friends than they did with their owners. I soon realized that all the animals had more to say and more opinions about life than I had ever imagined. I learned that dogs really wanted to dig in the dirt, get dirty and do dog things and that all the animals wanted to be respected for who they were. They did not want us to treat them as little people.

As I felt my way along in learning this new language, I felt that my skills were not improving as fast as I would have liked – but my human friends apparently believed otherwise. Friends started to send me photographs of horses. I would write down my information from reading the picture and return it with the photos, then learn from the owners how accurate my readings were. This gave me the confidence to start doing telephone readings: someone would call, give me the pet's name and I would answer the owner's questions, talk in general with the pet and finish the reading by scanning its body for physical problems.

As my confidence in my ability to talk with animals grew, my other life, in the horse business, had also grown. I had managed, in the space of five years, to build up my farm's clientele, work at the racetrack, gain experience as a Thoroughbred trainer, get divorced, remarry and become an animal communicator.

In my second marriage I learned that the Universe always provides for us, as well as the lesson: "When the student is ready a teacher appears." Tom, my husband, was a wonderful, knowledgeable horseman who entered my life when my mentor and teacher from the racetrack died. After his death I was feeling very lost and insecure when the Universe brought Tom into my life. He came to work as a manager on the farm, because my business had expanded past what I could handle with just myself and two employees. Tom had a background in all phases of the Thoroughbred as well as the American Saddlehorse world. I discovered immediately that he could talk with the animals much better than I could – a skill he said he learned from his Native American grandfather – tracing back to his family's Cherokee heritage.

Tom was the next step in raising my levels of awareness. Not only could he talk to animals, but he was also very connected to spirit. When we married, he brought with him his spirit guides, who soon became a large part of my life. It was during the early years of our marriage that I discovered the metaphysical world; pushed into it, I am sure, by one of Tom's guides, who told me her name was Proc. I started to read many books on metaphysical subjects, and guided by spirit I realized that there was more to the Universe than I could ever imagine. Our horse business kept growing, but Tom felt that my animal communication work did not need to be made public. We both felt our business would suffer if people knew I talked with their horses. The only animal communication work I did during this time was for my friends and horse trainers who accepted my abilities and sought out my help with their horses, dogs and cats or lost pets.

It was also during these years that I started helping friends search for pets that had been lost or stolen. The first lost dog that I looked for taught me many important lessons about how our animals view the world.

Misty lived in a country home with a large group of other dogs. Her owner was a "rescuer." There were many well-cared for and loved dogs here, but this particular dog had never made a strong link or connection to her humans at home. When she decided to leave the small farm where she was living, her life became one big adventure. I was able to see through her eyes where she was; around a schoolyard, by water and trees or walking down a sidewalk, just observing life as she went. She didn't seem to mind going through trash cans for food. To her, all these new places were fun. The owner's daughter and I searched for her for months. I received numerous phone calls confirming that the dog had been seen in the area I had described, but she would be gone before her human arrived. Eventually I could receive no more energy, pictures, or thoughts from her. I told the owner that Misty had no strong urge to go home. She had been happy there, but she wanted to see the world. I know that she eventually crossed into spirit without ever finding another home. This dog taught me that some animals are truly here for the adventure. They just want to experience life and live in the moment. This was not a dog who had suffered abuse or had any problems with people; she just loved being free to explore the world.

Misty's feelings were a new experience for me. Since dogs tend to be pack animals by instinct, I had always believed that humans and a human home could serve as a pack and that our job was to keep them safe and cared for. This dog gave me a wide range of feelings to explore. She was cautious outside her home environment but not afraid. She accepted conditions as they came and truly enjoyed her adventures. I know that she had no fears, and she certainly didn't fear death because she knew that death only meant a change in form and shape; that there was no end to life, just changes. She also made me realize how different each animal's personality is, and that they really want to be respected for who they are, just as we do. The final thing I learned from her was that the animals that want to get home are those that have developed the strongest connection with their humans. When I start to look for lost pets now, I first try to establish their feelings. How afraid are they, if at all? What are they thinking about – getting home or just living in the moment and letting the Universal energy move them? How they feel plays a large part in getting them home and keeping them tuned in to me.

Ruffy, the other dog I looked for at this time, showed me a different aspect of animal feelings and personalities. Ruffy taught me about the strong connections that animals develop, not only with their people, but with other animals. Ruffy belonged to close friends of mine, great animal lovers, who had a large group of horses, dogs, cats, birds, and other pets. She had a very strong connection to her human and animal family, but escaped from a racetrack tack room one afternoon while her owner, a horse trainer, was running a horse in a race. When someone opened the door she ran out, hoping to find her owner. However, as she later told me, she was quickly picked up by a man who kept her and made no effort to return her. When I was called to look for her, the owners had already searched for several days and had posted flyers and run ads offering a reward for her return.

The first pictures Ruffy sent me were the legs, in blue jeans, of a tall thin man. She also told me that she was in a small house or apartment with a small yard. I was never able to see the man's face but I felt he was very tall and thin. Ruffy also told me that the man kept her because he wanted a dog of her breed, a Jack Russell terrier. I assumed that the price for a registered dog was beyond this man's means. Ruffy also sent pictures to her dog friends at home and one of these dogs confirmed, by sending me pictures, that Ruffy was still safe and alive. After several weeks, the man felt safe enough to tie Ruffy outside when he went to work. In a few days she had chewed through the rope, and headed back in the direction of the racetrack where she had been lost. My friends were still posting flyers and "missing dog" ads, and they began to get phone calls reporting sightings of Ruffy. She eventually ended up in a cornfield close to the racetrack. When her owner arrived, he brought with him one of

21

the dogs from home. Ruffy came out of hiding when she recognized the other dog and her owner.

Each time I talked with Ruffy while she was lost, she showed me pictures of her home, her owner and her dog family and always indicated in her feelings how much she wanted to be with them again. This dog had such a strong link to her humans and the other dogs that her main desire was always to return. She had no wish to live on her own or experience the world outside of what she knew as her family and pack.

Ruffy's owners told me later that the most important thing I did for them was to give them hope that she would return by always telling them that she was still alive. This hope sustained them and kept them looking for her until they were reunited. I know that keeping our thoughts and feelings in the positive keeps all the doors open for the Universe to bring us good. When we let go of hope we fall back into the negative and close the doors, preventing the good from entering our lives.

Working with these two lost dogs not only gave me confidence in my sending and receiving of pictures, but it also helped me develop guidelines for the type of questions I ask to determine a pet's location. It taught me to be more aware of how each animal feels and what level of connection they have with the world around them. Like people, some want to experience all parts of life, while others are happy with what they have at home and have no desire to look farther.

CHAPTER 4
What I Learned from Working with Horses
and Other Animals

Life with my husband, and the rapid growth of our horse business, gave me experience with different breeds of horses and with many other species of animals.

Tom loved all animals, and we soon had pet goats, llamas, pigs, and donkeys, as well as ducks, geese, and swans. The new animal energies around me were a great source of happiness and gave me the opportunity to practice communication with a wider variety of animals.

Among all the changes came a new breed of horse for me to work with – the American Paint Horse. Tom introduced me to the breed, having first seen racing Paint horses when he worked as a horse trainer on a ranch in Colorado. American Paints can only have registered Quarter horse and Thoroughbred bloodlines mixed with their Paint blood. Their pedigrees make them very versatile horses and they do everything from being working ranch horses to racing. We purchased Paints that raced, as well as others for me to train as English type show horses. I found their personalities to be very different from those of the Thoroughbreds and Warmbloods I had worked with in the past. The Paints really liked people and wanted a job, whereas many of the Thoroughbreds only wanted to be pampered and cared for. I had found Thoroughbreds who wanted to please, but had never found a breed with such a strong work ethic. The Paints put a lot more effort into communicating. All the Paints I trained thought I was upset with them if I failed to ride or interact with them each day. The Thoroughbreds, with a few exceptions, had always been more aloof and self-absorbed.

Tom and I were so busy with the farm that after our horses were broken we sent them to trainers for training and racing. Whether they were Paints or Thoroughbreds, the horses always asked the same questions when I came to see them. It amazed me how similar their basic questions were. They asked about my employees. I would get pictures of a groom, then the feeling of missing him or her. The young horses usually sent me pictures of their mothers and asked whether they were still at the farm. Horses all know about being sold and for some of them this was a big issue. If we changed trainers, or if the trainers changed employees, the horses always sent me pictures of their new groom or rider.

The Paints would tell me about being bumped by other horses in a race, or that the condition of the track surface bothered them. Of course there were some horses, regardless of breed, who just didn't have the ability to be good racehorses and I had to ask them if they had another career in mind – from being show horses to pleasure horses.

The Thoroughbreds asked questions about grooms at the farm and other horses left behind at home, but they were never shy about expressing their fears to me. At times it was the fear of physical injury, like breaking a leg; other times it was leaving a horse friend by going to a new place or being sold. I soon realized that the people caring for them may have said, "If you run badly you will be sold," or they might have actually seen another horse suffer an injury on the racetrack. I had already realized how much the horses talked with each other at the farm, but working with their fears at the racetrack was new to me.

Each year I had sold some horses as yearlings to produce income for the farm. The young horses were always told that they would be sold and they generally looked upon it as a new adventure and challenge. The horses I raced were eventually going to return home and be bred or go into retirement. Having older horses racing really gave me a different insight into horses' minds. It was interesting to process their thoughts and see how I could explain real life off the farm to them.

Of all my Thoroughbred racehorses, two will always stand out in my mind – Charlie and Freddy. Charlie was two years old when my father died. He was in training but had developed a mysterious leg injury and was not sold in the dispersal sale with my father's horses. My trainer felt that he was a talented horse and wanted me to keep him and race him when he became physically sound again. Charlie returned from the racetrack, spent the winter at the farm, and whatever had been wrong with his hind leg vanished as mysteriously as it came. Charlie and I bonded quickly and it soon became clear how much confidence he had in his own ability to be a racehorse. Running was easy for him, and he took great pride in beating other horses and being the star of the barn. He would psych out his competition just like a human athlete. In the saddling paddock or in the starting gate I used to see him send pictures to his competition in the race. The pictures were always the same: Charlie racing in front of the group and staying in front to win the race. Charlie let me know that racing was his only job and he intended to do the best he could at all times. He won a large percentage of his races along with several stakes races before he retired to the farm. When asked if he wanted to be a regular riding horse, he sent only pictures of little people or jockeys on him. He told me he did miss his groom from the track, but he had very clear ideas of what he wanted. He was either a racehorse or a retired racehorse – nothing in between. He lived in retirement until the old age of twenty-seven when he told me his body was okay for an old horse but that he really wanted to go into spirit and be free of the body. He has never left me and now contacts me from spirit whenever he wants to.

Freddy was totally different. Charlie accepted, with no emotion, the fact that he was a racehorse, and by his quiet attitude and serious personality let me know that racing was a serious job. Freddy, however, was excitable and fun-loving, and lacked Charlie's intensity and focus. Freddy was broken to ride, and started his early training on my farm with me. When he went to the racetrack he was ready for the next step into a new adventure. As his levels of fitness improved he began to feel very good about himself. When I asked him how he felt before his first race, he responded by saying that he knew he would win. He ran well, but finished in third place. When I arrived

26

at the barn after the race, he was upset with me. He felt I had failed to make him aware of the big picture. He kept telling me how hard it was to run with all the other horses, about the surface of the track not feeling good to his feet, and the crowd noise – all conditions that cannot be duplicated in morning training. Freddy took everything personally, and he did a wonderful job of letting me know how frustrated he was with his first race. He had only a moderate amount of talent as a racehorse but he always tried his best. He certainly got the message to me that no matter how hard I tried I could not always give my horses everything they needed for the big picture of life after they left home. On the other hand, this horse made me very aware of his levels of communication and his understanding of all the small parts in his life. He showed me that the animals are capable of more reasoning in their thinking than I had ever realized.

As well as being with the horses, I fed and took care of the goats, llamas, and waterfowl on the farm. The variety of creatures Tom and I added to the farm gave me insight into a wide range of mentalities. We had a large lake and I was given a pair of geese who were a cross of white domestic geese and Canada geese. Other clients supplied us with a variety of ducks, and a pair of black swans. My afternoons consisted of feeding all my non-horse friends. Each winter, large flocks of Canada geese would stay on our lake and we kept a large supply of corn available for them. It was beautiful to watch them land and glide around the lake. One visiting pair learned to eat corn from my hands and returned each year. They always sent me the same picture – one of me feeding them – then they would send me pictures of their babies. The swans let everyone know, by body language as well as pictures, that they were in charge of the lake.

Other than the Canada geese, my favorites were the white ducks. They followed me for food, and I enjoyed watching them swim and bob up and down in the water. All the waterfowl had basically the same energy: they were very group-oriented, as they were bred to be, but all of them expressed to me how free they felt and how happy they were to just be living in the moment.

The llamas gave me insight into true herd mentality. My breeding pair, Tony and Lilly, had come from a breeder of exotic animals. Both were young, a year to a year and a half old. Tony had spent several months in a petting zoo and Lilly had been sold as a baby but returned to the breeder when her human family moved and they could no longer keep her. In spite of some handling and socializing, both llamas always made it clear that they really wanted to be left alone and that they wanted to be with large groups of llamas. Their breeder would never sell just one llama and it was easy for me to see why – they just weren't happy away from their own kind. Lilly sent me pictures of huge herds of llamas – a horse farm in Kentucky was not where she wanted to be. The llamas were kind, never spit on people and were fairly friendly, but their herd mentality did not allow me to establish the link or closeness that I liked to have with my animals. Talking with them reminded me of talking with the cattle on our farm. Their primary focus was the rest of the herd.

The goats were the most fun for me. I started with one pair of Nubian crossbred females, named Gertrude and Hildy. They came to the farm when they were about six months old – we discovered them while we were horse shopping on a neighboring farm. Once they realized that I could speak their language, they expected me to play with them as if I were another goat. This always included, for them, running and jumping in the air, but stopping before they butted me. Their favorite game consisted of me sitting on the ground while they rubbed their heads on my back and arms – if I could talk to them, they expected me to have the same smell. My goats were very happy, and I spent many hours playing with them and simply trying to be in the moment with them.

Our first group of donkeys started with two jennys from the Bureau of Land Management adoption program. They had been completely wild until rescued from the Grand Canyon area in Arizona. One of them was pregnant and so we eventually had another long-ears to care for. They became quite people-oriented over the years. Their job was just to be "cute" and they had no problem being wonderful companions on the farm. They adapted to farm life and were happy with each other and happy with the horses. They never gave me the feeling that anything was missing in their life and never expressed any fears or problems. The baby grew up to be very people-friendly, and eventually assumed the job of being a companion to different horses on the farm.

Living and caring for all of these animals gave me a greater understanding of animals' minds. Understanding what they wanted and liked expanded my thinking and awareness. They taught me to be open to a variety of experiences, all seen from the animal's point of view.

CHAPTER 5

The Spiritual Side of My Work

This wonderful, expansive growth period lasted for almost eleven years. I continued to practice animal communication wherever I went. In these years Tom and I traveled to horse sales and horse races in other states. We also visited Thoroughbred and Paint farms and ranches. At times we went to see our own horses race or to buy horses for our farm. All of this traveling gave me a wonderful opportunity to talk with all types of horses. Some we had raised, while others were new to us.

The new horses always responded quickly with pictures of where they lived, their horse friends or people who were around them, and gave me feelings about their work. On the whole, most of the young horses were looking for adventure and fun; they enjoyed training for the races and horse shows. At horse sales, the young horses were anxious to take in all the events happening around them, and looked forward to a new part of life. The older horses that I talked to gave me impressions of how their lives had been. What seemed most important to them were compatible horse friends and owners who spent time with them. If their owners weren't present they generally attached themselves to their grooms or trainers, but most of them knew who their owners were.

As more animals and people came and went in my life, my spiritual awareness continued to grow. It would have been difficult to expand as an animal communicator without exploring all the creative and spiritual forces around me. The longer Tom and I were together, the more important his spirit guides became in my life. It didn't occur to me to ask anyone who my own guides or angels were. I just accepted his helpers as my own, tried to listen to them and went on working with animals.

In working with animals, I had also seen and communicated with those that had crossed into spirit. One of my own dogs, Tessie, came to me minutes after my vet called to break the news to me of her death from autoimmune disease. She appeared in the body of her younger days, looking about a year old. She had come to tell me that she was leaving this plane. She told me good-bye and said that she was on her way. She asked me to tell Linn, one of her best human friends, good-bye.

On another occasion I was looking for a friend's lost dog when the dog appeared to me from spirit. This time the dog showed me beautiful emerald green grass and brilliant blue sky. I knew immediately, from the vivid colors, that she was in spirit and she wanted to let us know that she had passed on. I was learning about life after what we call "death," but the animals made it plain that although their body shape, age, and place of residence might change, they did not die.

It was a great shock when my husband told me that he was "going to die." He expressed regrets at leaving me, said how much he loved me but that it was time for him to move on. I denied his words, refused to believe him and tried to ignore what he had told me. One month later Tom crossed into spirit while he slept. I was devastated to lose the only person that I counted on and loved. I had no family, but all my friends came to be with me and console me. Most of my close friends were also on their own spiritual paths, and each one told me a very similar story – anywhere from twenty-four to forty-eight hours before Tom crossed into spirit, they were given the message or strong intuitive feeling that I needed them and that they had to contact me immediately. Eventually, through my friends' stories about the hours before his death, and in talking with Tom's guides, I realized that this was part of the Universal plan for me and that there are no accidents.

Tom's death pushed me to face my biggest fears, but opened the door to a greater level of spiritual and animal communication. My two biggest fears were living alone, and being in charge of two farms, a cattle farm and a horse farm. I had always depended on Tom to look after the farm machinery, take care of the cattle, grow the hay and corn for the livestock to eat and do the major day-to-day farm and horse chores. I had worked with him for years, but we had divided the responsibilities between us. I was not afraid to live in a house alone; my fear was having to face the emptiness left by the lack of a partner to share my life.

My human friends did everything they could to help me take charge of the day-to-day life and farm chores, while my spirit guides cared for the other parts of me. On the day of Tom's crossing I asked his guides to tell me what I was supposed to do; to give me some insight into where I should go now. They responded with pictures and thoughts; and, since I have always been clairvoyant (to see) and clairaudiaunt (to hear), it was like seeing a small motion picture in my head. I was climbing over giant boulders (not going around them) on a rocky mountain path. Intuitively, I knew the boulders represented the new challenges in my life, and Tom's guides told me that I would be helping people. Until then I had assumed that my work would always be restricted to animals, but now I was clearly told that it was to include both animals and people.

My close contact with spirit introduced new guides into my life – my own family of guides, who at this time were always Native American. It was a great comfort in the next years to feel their presence around me, to ask them questions and know that they would always give me answers. Exactly one month after Tom's transition I received a message from my guides that I would live alone for six years. I responded that I would die from being alone that long. In their infinitely patient manner, they assured me that I could and would survive and that I was to take this time to prepare for the next part of my life.

The next few years were filled with my true spiritual quest: having readings from intuitives, which verified the information from my guides, reading books on metaphysical subjects, and learning about spirit. This new information directed me to more books and finally to human teachers – those who taught me meditation, healers who showed me energy balancing and one who helped me with my past life regressions. In my healing, I found that the past life regressions were very important. As I meditated, I saw other lives where I had been a highly respected teacher, while many – especially my Native American lives – focused on my love and connection with animals. Finally, I saw lives that focused on past relationships with my family and friends.

As I went through these changes, a new group of friends came into my life. Here were people who acknowledged the spiritual aspects of their lives just the way I did. Together we explored what spirit and the Universe wanted us to do.

As I progressed on my new path, my animal communication became more important. I no longer kept my readings in the background. Horse trainers asked me to go to barns and work with their clients' horses. Eventually, these clients expressed a desire to learn to talk with their own horses, dogs and cats. Taught by my guides, I began to develop a method to teach this new language. My first workshops were held at clients' homes and barns, but eventually I began doing yearly workshops at my own farm. At the same time I was constantly refining my teaching methods and learning how to organize my workshops.

The biggest surprise for me was my guides' announcement that I had to start reading for people, too. Until I turned to them for guidance after Tom's crossing, it had never occurred to me that "people readings" were part of the plan. When I expressed reluctance, I was told that the pets would bring people to me and that I would answer questions about spirit and give direction for the humans.

I had visited a small local psychic fair to buy books and have readings for myself. These readings confirmed the messages from my guides and also turned up new information about parts of my future, like the television, radio shows, and lectures, and all the traveling that would eventually come. They also gave me a different perspective on where my life might go if I could continue on my spiritual path for the next few years. I reserved a reader's place at a future fair as an animal communicator and reader of Native American tarot cards. My guides had picked out my deck of cards and worked with me on the interpretation of each card. At the first fair, I did more people readings than pet readings and felt I was really on my way into a new life.

The managers at small shows usually asked their readers to do a lecture. All the lectures were free, and I volunteered to lecture on pets and animal communication. These lectures gave me the experience I would later need to work with large groups of people, and greater insight into what people wanted in my workshops. After the first fair I began traveling to different states to work as an intuitive reader. My previous travel had mostly been to compete in horse shows – now I left my farm so that I could participate in a different type of event.

I had been fortunate to develop a wonderful support system of excellent, responsible employees for my farm, and was able to travel knowing that the farm and horses were being well cared for. However, my guides were making it clear that I would eventually have to sell my farm and give up being a horse trainer so that I could start the work that the Universe had planned for me. It took me several years and many bumps in the road before I could release such an important part of my past. I had always felt responsible for the well-being of my employees, but as the Universe made changes in their lives and they moved off in new directions it was easier for me to let go of my life on the farm. At last I felt I was starting to see a big picture, and closed my farm with few regrets. The Universe had allowed me to experience many years with my horses. I felt very happy and knew that I reached the goals I had set for myself as a horse trainer. I let go of the past and jumped into the new life that was planned for me.

Since then, I have traveled to all parts of the country. I have worked at large Expos giving lectures, answering questions and doing readings for pets and people. I have also traveled to horse shows and dog events where I do readings for the animals that are competing, as well as working with their trainers to help them understand all aspects of the horse or dog's personality. Fortunately, horse trainers have always accepted me because I can speak the language of horsemen as well as that of their horses. My travels also include going to different areas and conducting workshops where I teach animal communication. I believe that anyone can learn to speak this language. You don't have to be psychic or have any special gift – you just need the desire to do it.

CHAPTER 6

My Dogs – My Teachers

During the years before I left the farm to focus on my work as an animal psychic, the Universe began to prepare me for this new role by connecting me with a long succession of wonderful animals. Among the most memorable of these were my dogs Blackberry, Sunshine, and Joe Dog.

When Blackberry entered my life I had just started to work with animal communication. She gave me insight into the intuitive traits and pack orientation of the dog world. Her mother belonged to a pack of wild dogs that sometimes lived on our eight hundred acre farm and terrorized my barn cats. Most of the land was used for raising crops and grazing herds of cattle, affording the wild dogs plenty of places to hide. I practiced free-feeding of my barn cats, leaving open bags of cat food in the barns. This encouraged feral cats, raccoons, skunks – and finally the dog pack – to enter my barns at night. Eventually the dog pack went from eating the cat food to a mass killing of barn cats. This attack was followed by another, and we began to worry that the small calves or foals might be the next victims.

My farm employees agreed the only way to approach the dog problem was to wait outside the barns and shoot guns over the dogs' heads as they came to the barn. Our goal was to scare them away rather than kill them. The plan worked. When the guns fired, the dogs ran back toward the cornfields where we had seen them living. In pursuing the dogs, my husband chased them toward a nearby tobacco barn. He stopped abruptly as he heard what seemed to be a dog screaming in pain. Afraid that one of the dogs had been shot by accident and was badly hurt, he entered the barn and turned on the lights. There sat a small, terrified black puppy between four and six weeks old. Apparently her mother had left her in the tobacco barn while the pack was making its run through the horse barn. In the rush to run to safety, the puppy was left behind by the older dogs. He picked up the screaming puppy, put her in his truck and brought her home. He had no idea if her mother would return for her, and felt she needed to be cared for. Since I had always adopted all the homeless animals that came to me I took Blackberry in with no negative thoughts about her family. I named her Blackberry because she was solid black, and appeared to be completely untamed. I took her inside the house and she spent the night in the guest bathroom. Apparently having my other dogs in the same house comforted her, because she quickly stopped crying and went to sleep. The dogs awakened me at daylight with a volley of barking. Outside our fenced yard was Blackberry's mother with two other female dogs from the pack. She made it very obvious that she wanted her puppy returned to her. The mother looked like a Border collie in size and shape, while her companions were more nondescript. For at least half an hour, they ran around the yard, trying to find a way in through the high board and wire fence. These were dogs with no connections to people, and several hours earlier men had been chasing them, firing shots over their heads. Yet they had tracked this puppy over two miles and knew that she was inside my house. I felt it was safer for Blackberry to grow up with me than be returned to her mother. Life in a pack of wild dogs often resulted in early deaths, from farmers shooting them or starvation. It felt wrong to return such a sweet and kind puppy to a life of uncertainty and fear. Eventually the three dogs gave up, but returned each morning for several days still trying to rescue the puppy.

Blackberry adapted to domestic life immediately. I knew that having my two adult dogs, Smokey, a German shepherd and Tessie, a Catahoula, offered her security and a new pack to belong to. Her personality remained reserved, but never too shy, and she acted like any other puppy I had raised. The wild dogs did not return to the barns and we began to wonder if they had left the farm completely. Blackberry seemed very happy and adjusted quickly to her new home. She had been living with me about four weeks when her mother returned with a big surprise for me. My large horse van was parked between the house and the horse barn. Walking to the barn one morning, I saw several puppies run under the van. The mother dog had brought the rest of her litter for me to raise. I was never sure whether Blackberry had sent her messages of happiness and a secure life or whether the mother had decided for herself that I could give a secure home to her little ones. Unfortunately, these puppies were at least ten to twelve weeks old and were not at all friendly. I was able to coax all four of them from under the horse van by luring them with food. When they came out to eat I grabbed each one by the back of the neck, in the same way that a mother dog would pick up her pups. Then I placed each one in a dog crate and moved them to a large stall in the nearest horse barn. I started trying to hand feed them, spend time with them, and hoped that they would learn to trust me. After two weeks I took them to our local animal shelter, in the hope that some of them might be adopted and make good companions for someone. In follow-up phone calls I was told that all four of the puppies were adopted, but I never learned how their lives turned out.

Blackberry's mother stayed in touch. Although the pack of dogs avoided the barns, she returned at least once a month until the fall to see her puppy and check on her progress. She and her two friends would run around the outside of our yard fence. If Blackberry was outside she would run up and greet them. Then the wild dogs would leave and trot off toward the back of the farm. Her visits continued at intervals for several years. She never came alone – always with the same two companions. As my ability to do nonverbal communication grew I attempted to ask Blackberry how she felt about her family visits. She always acknowledged her mother, but I never picked up any feelings or thoughts that she wanted to know her better. The mother always sent me strong feelings of love surrounding her puppies, and she felt that I represented a form of safety and security for the young dogs not yet skilled in living on their own.

When Blackberry was four years old, her mother brought me yet another puppy to raise. Tom saw her first, walking through the field with a yellow puppy in her mouth. She trotted in the back door of our training barn and put the puppy in one of the horse stalls. Then she waited outside the stall until she saw Tom enter the barn. She made sure he picked up the puppy then she ran out the back door. We never saw her again. This puppy looked exactly like a yellow Labrador retriever, and in contrast to Blackberry's shyness, she had a strong outgoing disposition. We named her Sunshine, for her yellow color and warm personality. I eventually gave her to my mother and watched as she grew into a large, fun-loving, happy dog.

Blackberry was one of my practice dogs during the years that I worked on animal communication. My other two dogs would send me feelings and thoughts, while Blackberry sent out pictures. She was fourteen years old the summer I left my farm in Lexington to move to a new farm in Paris, Kentucky. Blackberry passed into spirit just before the move as she slept in the front yard of the old farm.

Sunshine lived with my mother until my mother crossed into spirit. She returned to live the rest of her life with Tom and I, and she went to spirit one month before Tom did. During the years that she and Blackberry lived in my home together they never became friends, nor did they acknowledge any type of family relationship. Sunshine kept her outgoing personality but always kept looking for my mother. She told me that no one ever really died, and that she kept expecting my mother to return to visit her. Blackberry always kept her reserved personality and enjoyed the company of our cats and dogs much more than that of people.

I found it very interesting to compare these two dogs. Sunshine and Blackberry had the same mother and both began their lives in a wild dog pack, but each had a different personality. Blackberry was closely connected to me, but she preferred dog friends to humans. Sunshine arrived with a fun-loving, confident personality. She treated everyone she met as a friend and looked at the world as a wonderful place for her to play. Both dogs started life with no human companions, and I enjoyed watching them grow into happy, secure dogs. Observing their differences, I realized that all dogs are individuals regardless of where they come from.

The wild dog pack brought one more loving dog spirit into my family. Ten years after Blackberry's arrival, Joe entered my life. He was a large, muscular black and tan Doberman with uncut ears. His floppy ears gave him a hound dog look. By the time he came to me I was proficient in animal communication, and my ability to speak to him helped us get together. By now, the dog pack included several lost dogs. When we saw them on the farm, several were wearing collars. This time it was my herd of goats and the cattle being chased and terrorized by the dogs. We had seen the dogs during the fall, but when the weather turned to true cold winter they would come into a horse barn and sleep in empty stalls at night. When we entered the barn at 5:00 a.m. to feed the horses the dogs were usually gone. One morning Tom surprised them and shut the open stall doors, trapping all of them in our broodmare barn. It had been our plan to catch them, call the Humane Society and have them taken away. Joe was in a stall all by himself, and we learned that he was not a true member of the pack. The true wild dogs dug through the dirt in the stall floor and quickly escaped, but Joe sat in his stall and waited to see what would come next. We gave him water and food, but otherwise left him alone. After several days I asked him if I could come in and look at his collar and I.D. tag. He showed me pictures of me touching his collar so I went in to see if he could be identified and returned to his owner. The collar had no nameplate and his rabies tag contained only a number, without the name of a veterinary clinic. We kept him in the stall for several days until I felt that he was secure enough to ride to our house in the farm truck.

Blackberry and Sunshine welcomed him quickly. I had prepared them for his arrival by explaining that he was lost, needed a home, and would stay with us until I found his family for him. We had seen him running with the pack for at least three months, but I still wanted to try and return him to his first home. Then I asked the dogs and my cats what they wanted to name him. He had not been able to communicate anything about his name or home to me. The cats decided to call him Joe; or actually, Joe-Dog. They both told me that dogs, in their opinion, needed plain names while cats needed fancy names. So Joe-Dog joined our family while I attempted to find his own family. My vet told me his rabies tag was one used by the state of Kentucky at low-cost vaccination days. The state would charge a nominal fee and provide low-cost shots for all small animals several days a month during the summer. The numbers on the tags were not recorded and there were no ownership records kept. I advertised in the "found" section of the local paper but received no response. In no time Joe had become such an important member of my family that I didn't want to think of sending him off to his other home.

As we got to know each other, Joe became more open about the life he had before he was lost. He carefully related to me, with very clear images, the following information – that he lived in an apartment (it looked like a two-story building in a complex of similar buildings). His owners were an African American family with three boys (two appeared to be in their early teens, while the other boy looked much younger). Joe spent most of his time inside and was an only dog. He also conveyed to me that his first name was Mike or Michael, but that he was pleased with the name Joe. When I asked how he became separated from his family I saw pictures of him running from a park or recreation area into a group of houses in what appeared to be a subdivision. From that point on he was really lost and eventually kept moving until he was on farmland. He had no sense of direction and I doubt that he had ever been loose or out of his immediate neighborhood before. I had felt that Joe had lived fairly close to my farm, but he apparently had no idea about which direction he had come from.

Several years later, he was riding in the car with me when I took a shortcut from the main highway into Lexington. This route took us through a subdivision and passed by a group of apartments, then past a school and on to another road. I immediately picked up a feeling of instant recognition from him that I was in his old neighborhood. Completely by accident I had discovered that Joe had grown up no more than three miles from my home.

Joe's only quirk was his eating habits. For almost a year he asked for only sliced white bread to eat. He told me that that was essentially all he had to eat at his other home. It was over a year before he would eat dry dog food. He told me that his diet had been bread and table scraps at his other home and the dog food didn't taste good to him.

Joe's ability to reason and tell me about his former family life surpassed that of most dogs I talked to. My own dogs had always lived in the moment. They could go back to the past if I asked them but they concentrated on the here and now. Joe sent pictures of a lonely life as a puppy. He spent what seemed to him most of his first years alone in an apartment. He went outside on a leash but he had really wanted to play, run and be "special," as he put it in his own words. I knew that he had received some good basic obedience training. He would heel, sit, stay and would never leave the porch of our house without permission. He yearned to be a puppy again, and always wished that he could have spent his puppyhood playing on the farm and being my dog. All of these feelings came with pictures of me playing with him while he was in a small puppy body.

After Blackberry, Sunshine and R.T., my cat, went to spirit Joe started asking me for a puppy. He wanted a puppy that looked just like him – another Doberman. One year after Tom's death I did get a new puppy for us – Berrie, a Scottish terrier. She was not the size Joe wanted, but he was thrilled to have her at home with us. I had also known for several months that Joe had cancer. He had been slowing down but he was between ten and twelve years of age. As Berrie became more demanding, Joe tried to keep up with her, but found it too difficult. He confided to me that he was happy I had finally gotten him a puppy, but he was really glad there was only one puppy at home for him to take care of. Joe went into spirit three months after Berrie came to live with us. I have been told by my spirit guides that this kind, loving dog reincarnated after several years in spirit. I hope this time he found the active, happy life he deserved here on earth.

Because Joe came into my life at a time when I had become very proficient with nonverbal communication, it was easy to send out pictures, ask him a question, and receive a return image and feeling. Living with Joe added a new layer and texture to my work as an animal communicator. From Joe I got first-hand experience with his thoughts and feelings. It showed me again how the Universe sends us teachers from the most unlikely sources. I don't think he missed his first home after he moved in with me but he occasionally sent me pictures of the boys with a feeling that he wondered what they were doing. He always let me know how scared and unhappy he was with the dog pack. These dogs had been shot at by farmers, whose cattle they chased, and Joe's x-rays showed buckshot in his back and hind legs. They had very little to eat and he wanted a home with humans, but he didn't know how to leave the pack and find a friendly person.

Dogs and horses had told me before that they missed their mothers and the first humans they had lived with, but Joe went deeper. He sent me worried feelings when he saw me riding or working with my horses, and when Tom died he was devastated. All of our horses, dogs, and cats viewed Tom as the leader of the pack. When he died the horses accepted me quickly as herd boss or pack leader, but Joe always felt we needed a new man in our lives. Joe would send me pictures of men who came to the house or farm, with his feelings about which one could live with us. However, he was not able to reason out all the parts in this situation. While none of the men were candidates in my eyes, Joe would give me his opinions on each of them: for example, "really doesn't like dogs." Another man might move too fast for him, or one might talk too loudly. He finally did settle on one man – a kind, friendly horse trainer, already married, who loved my dogs and horses. Joe would often tell me, by sending pictures of this man in our house, that if he moved in with us we would be happy again. Joe had his own insight on our life but watching him reason with problems, experience his grieving when Tom died and take my emotional pain into his body were all new experiences for me in relating to and understanding the animals. This dog was able to reason, feel and express his feelings on a level that I had not experienced before. He introduced me to working with animals on a deeper and more spiritual level than I ever believed possible.

CHAPTER 7

My Cats – My Teachers

My own animal stories would be incomplete without my cats. Members of the feline world made a late entry into my life. My mother was allergic to them, so living with cats had to wait until I left home and had my own house. It didn't take the Universe long to start sending cats to me. Within three months of being in my own home, cats appeared at the door. My first was a very sick gray and white barn kitten. I rescued her, brought her home and started learning how to take care of cats. This small kitten received the name "Watch Kitty" because she was always under my feet when I walked through the house. Next came R.T. (short for Rudy Tooty). He was another barn kitten, abandoned by his mother, that I raised on a bottle. We had to teach him to eat solid food and instruct him on how to go up and down steps.

R.T. always lived his life as a cat to the very fullest and took great pride in his skills as a hunter. He would go outside, catch a field mouse, bring it in and hide it in my riding boots. I eventually learned to turn my boots upside down and shake them out before I put them on. On one memorable occasion he caught and killed three field mice in our house (we did live in the country) then neatly arranged them in a row – on my side of the bed, so I would see them when I got up.

R.T. also became Joe-Dog's best friend. They would sleep in my bed together or curl up on Joe's dog bed and nap in the kitchen. As R.T. aged, he became aware of how limited his time was with me. He told me that he would stay on this plane as long as he felt like hunting and being active but he had no intention of being sickly or dependent on me in his last days. In June, about two months before Tom died, R.T. conveyed the thought to me that he was planning to leave his body. He had no big physical problems, but he was sixteen years old and I knew that his body was starting to wear out. By the end of June he had stopped hunting and going outside. Most of his time was spent sleeping in the kitchen or just sitting looking out the window watching birds and squirrels play in our yard. Then he gave me a very surprising message. He showed me pictures of my friend Mary who visited us each July from her home in Florida. R.T. wanted to see Mary one last time and tell her good-bye.

When Mary called me with her schedule for her trip to Kentucky, I told her about R.T.'s desire to see her before he left his body. By the time she came to visit in July R.T. was at the point where eating and sleeping were his only activities. Mary came directly from the airport to my house to see R.T. He sat on the sofa with her, let her stroke him, and regained some of his old energy. After she left he retired to his bed in the kitchen and went to sleep. From that sleep, his breathing slowed and he passed into a coma. It took about twenty-four hours for his body to give up and stop functioning. I knew he had willed himself out of his body after he went to sleep. All of us, Tom, Joe and I respected his wishes and let him leave us in the way he had requested. His little cat body was buried in the garden with the bodies of my other pet friends.

It was several years before R.T. contacted me from spirit and it was again in a most unusual way. I was in New York City attending a workshop conducted by Brian Weiss and James Van Praagh. Brian Weiss was leading us in a group meditation designed to introduce us to our spirit guides on the other side. As we proceeded down steps into a garden we would find a guide waiting for us. As I went through the gate into the garden I was met by R.T. and Smokey, my German shepherd who had lived with us when R.T. was a kitten. They both greeted me, then explained that they were now my guides. They had returned to assist me in my work as an animal communicator. Their new job was to help me in the mediumship area of my work. When I wanted to contact a pet in spirit it became their job to find that specific animal spirit and lead it to me.

Along with R.T. two other cats stand out as special friends – Morgan and Mollie. Morgan came from our local Humane Society as a small, unhealthy six-week-old kitten. In 1986, my sense of loss following my mother's death was deepened when I lost Smokey, my German shepherd, and Watch Kitty, my first cat, within just a few months of mother's passing. To fill the huge holes left by the departures of my dog and cat I decided to get a new kitten. Because our Humane Society had taken in so many of the animals that I had rescued, I felt that I should rescue from them for a change. When the animal shelter opened on a Sunday afternoon in September I was there to pick out my kitten. The attendant told me at the main desk

51

that very few kittens were available. Most of the cats were adults looking for new homes. I knew beforehand that I wanted a black and white female kitten, but it sounded as if I might be out of luck. When I walked to the cat section of the building I passed a window containing a box of sleeping kittens. One kitten was standing up in the box tapping a front paw on the window saying, "Here I am. Pick me, pick me." I stopped, looked at the number on her collar and went back to the front desk to tell them that I had found my kitten. Because of their young age the young woman volunteer was not sure that litter of kittens was eligible for adoption. To my relief they were old enough to leave, and Morgan came home with me on the first day she had been put up for adoption. She was so small and thin that I felt a fancy name would help her self-image, so her full name became Morgan Fairchild, named for the glamorous television actress. Morgan Fairchild's book about her life and her transformation from an ugly duckling to a beautiful television star had just been published and I felt she had the perfect name for my new kitten.

When Morgan arrived at my house I already had three dogs, two cats and a very tolerant husband living with me. In spite of her youth and small size Morgan attempted to dominate, or at least retrain, all our other pets. After three days of causing constant upset harassing the grown-up animals, Morgan left the house to try a new life as my office cat. Her new job meant having my large farm office, which doubled as a guest house, all to herself. I worked in my office every day, but essentially she would be undisturbed by other cats or dogs and could really rule with an iron paw, or however she viewed her queenly status. This new situation worked well for everyone. The pets at home settled down again and Morgan became my constant companion when I worked at my desk. As she grew older she could leave the office and explore the areas around the barns.

When I lived in the country all my cats were barn cats, or what I called inside/outside cats. They were vaccinated, spayed or neutered and they chose what type of life they wanted to lead on the farm. All of the cats were relatively safe; at that time we had no coyotes, wild dogs or any other predators to endanger their lives. Morgan chose to be an inside/outside cat, preferring the inside only in winter. After the first of January I started staying up all night to watch our foaling mares, standing by ready to act as midwife. I observed the pregnant mares on a closed circuit television monitor in my office. Morgan would wait for me to arrive each night and sit with me while we waited for new foals to be born. As the foaling season moved into spring I found it harder and harder to stay awake. If I dozed off she would gently tap my hand or arm with one small, black-and-white paw. If that failed to wake me she walked on my arm or jumped on my body. She knew keeping me up was a big part of her job as office cat. She also claimed the responsibility of guarding and watching over the barns, office and parking area on the front of the farm. At that time we had over four hundred acres, but Morgan established her territory and watched only the front buildings. Her territory included the parking area for the employees' cars and trucks. She would patrol the parking lot every morning, then keep track of each person as they left the parking area and walked to the barn office to punch in on the time clock. One new employee became Morgan's victim. When Terri arrived for work and left her truck, Morgan would attack like a dog, slapping at her heels with her paws and trying to jump up her leg while Terri ran from the parking lot with Morgan chasing her. When I asked Morgan why she had chosen her as a victim Morgan replied that it was fun to hear her yell. I felt that the main delight for Morgan was simply the thrill of the chase. In self-defense, Terri started bribing Morgan with donuts. When the offering was a yeast donut, Morgan let her pass. If it was only a cake donut or some other bite of food, she rejected it and the chase was on.

Morgan also patrolled the barn lofts, walking across high beams and the railings of the old tobacco barns that had been converted to horse barns. I would look up and see her fifteen to twenty feet in the air, dancing on the narrow rails as she walked from one side of the barn loft to the other. She also climbed trees and ran out on the limbs to chase the squirrels higher up in the tree. Again, when I asked why she did these gymnastics she simply said, "It's fun."

When I moved from Lexington to Paris, Morgan was forced to decide where she wanted to live at the new farm. In Lexington she did not have to share anything with the barn cats; she had the office to herself and was the queen. In Paris the office was moved into my house, so Morgan chose to stay in the main barn with the option of moving into my house if she chose to. Her gymnastic feats continued, and I would see her walking on the barn roof gutters or around the top edge of an unused water storage tank. Age didn't faze her and she kept on exploring all the high places. That spring she told me that she wanted to walk to the back of our new farm to see the neighbor's black and white Holstein cattle because, she said, "They look like me" and she was curious. When she failed to return that afternoon I began to worry. She had never left before and I knew something was wrong. Tom was out of town, and, in a panic, like any pet owner, I was having no luck in reaching my cat with nonverbal thoughts. I drove around the farm, and sent employees to look in all the places I thought she might be. When she was not found I became more upset than ever. I started calling the adjoining farms, describing Morgan and asking the farms to call me if she showed up at their house or barns. All the neighbors told me the same thing: "she was probably killed by a coyote," and, "why are you so upset about a cat?" This gave me some insight into the consciousness of the new area I lived in, but I knew she was still alive. After several days I calmed down enough to receive her messages. Yes, she was fine, but she was trapped in a building and couldn't get out. She told me that it had started to rain while she was looking at the cattle so she took refuge in what she thought was a farm storage building in the next field. It turned out to be a garage next to a small tenant house on a neighbor's farm. She was found by the tenant's children, taken to their house in the belief that she was a stray cat, and fastened up in the house. They would not let her out because they didn't want her to run away. She kept assuring me she was fine, and I started to look for the house. I knew the direction and had a good idea how far it was from my home, but failed to find it. All my newspaper ads and flyers went unanswered, but Morgan kept telling me she was fine and would be home when she could get out. Six weeks later she appeared at my kitchen door. Finally the new family had thought she was secure enough to stay with them and had let her outside. When she was free she ran the two miles home. I eventually saw the small farm house where she had been taken. It was under a hill and well hidden by trees. The only time the house could be seen was in winter when no leaves were on the trees. After this Morgan assured me that she would not leave our barn area again. One big adventure was more than enough for her.

When Tom died that August, Morgan had to make another decision on where to live. My house cat R.T. had gone to spirit one month before Tom. With R.T. gone and Tom gone I asked Morgan for the second time in her life to help me heal after deaths in my family. She agreed to leave the barn and be a house cat. Her new job was to be my companion, stay in the house and help Joe-Dog look after me. Morgan agreed on the condition that she be allowed to go outside and hunt, but only in my yard, whenever she wanted to. I agreed and she once again took on a new job. Morgan adjusted very quickly to her role as house cat and companion. She was older, and she enjoyed sleeping in bed, preferring to have a guest room all to herself.

Two years after Tom's death Mollie, a Manx cat, came to live with us. By now Joe-Dog had died and Morgan only had to share the house with Berrie, my Scottish terrier. Mollie proved from her first days with me to be a very special cat. She was dark brown with a beautiful gold spot on her forehead and gold spots on her hind feet. I was still in a deep depression after Tom's death when one of my friends gave her to me as a kitten, thinking that a new cat would help me regain some of my lost energy and balance. I rejected the gift and sent the kitten off to the barn. On the second day in the training barn she was accidentally locked up in a storage cabinet. When I couldn't find her she told me exactly where she was. Feeling very guilty, I quickly carried her back to my house so she could meet Morgan and Berrie. Berrie was thrilled to have a playmate, while Morgan told me that Mollie was an unusual cat and would be full of surprises for me. Mollie was a handful – a brown ball of energy. She and Berrie played tag in the house, then Mollie would play mountain lion and jump on Berrie's back from a couch or chair. In the meantime no suitable name came to me for our new kitten, so one night I asked her what name she wanted. She was so young I really didn't expect an answer but she quickly said, "You can call me Little Mollie. That's what the other man called me." I asked the friend who gave Mollie to me to confirm her name with her breeder, and he verified that it had indeed been Little Mollie. In no time she became the bright spot in our house. Her rough play with Berrie, her antics of flying off furniture, and finally the way she sat on the back of the couch and put her arm on my neck to keep me company while I watched television proved to me how understanding and intuitive she was. All her games made me laugh, and our quiet time provided me with a new spirit to talk to. Mollie told me about her past lives – some in Egypt as a cat, others as a mountain lion – and her experiences in astral travel. Morgan had been right, Mollie was not an average cat.

When Mollie was almost two years old, Morgan got in bed with me and confided how happy she was that Mollie was growing up. She went on to explain that Mollie had come to help me grow spiritually and teach me on my spiritual path. Morgan, on the other hand, really just wanted to be a cat. She wanted to hunt, sleep in warm places and enjoy life. She had selflessly become my companion and helped me heal emotionally when Tom died, but with Mollie growing up Morgan was relieved of her job as "a spiritual cat." Morgan has always remained a loyal friend and companion but she was ready to return to her life as a regular cat.

Mollie answered spiritual questions, took me with her on travels out of our bodies and moved my psychic energy up several levels. Before she was a year old she told me that we would travel to far places together. I thought she meant out of body travel, but as the years went on I realized that she knew we would travel across the country together when the time came to leave Kentucky.

Unhappily for me, when it was time to sell our farm and leave Kentucky for Arizona, Morgan chose not to travel with me. She reminded me that she was fifteen years old, and did not want to ride several days in a car; but most importantly, she wanted to stay on a farm in Kentucky where she could hunt and see horses and cattle. I found a home for her with a friend who lets her continue her life as an inside/outside cat. She tells Mollie and me that she is very happy, and has a new job. She is with another human who needs emotional healing. In her words, "He really needs me and you are fine now." She had so much experience helping me heal emotionally I know she is doing a wonderful job with her new person. If that job ends I have some other friends who promise to let her continue her cat life on their farms in Kentucky.

The presence of cats in my family brought me emotions and behaviors completely different from that of my dogs. The cats could be aloof, but when they felt I needed them they became like old friends expressing feelings of love and understanding. R.T., Mollie, and Morgan were very opinionated in choosing cat, dog or human friends but never failed to let me know that their relationship with me was special. My dogs' lives revolved around me and their farm activities. While my cats were occupied with their own lives, they never failed to come to me when they felt I needed love or companionship.

CHAPTER 8

A Special Gift

Not all my animals have been sent to help me heal or to be my teachers. When Frazier, my first adopted greyhound, entered my life the Universe let me know that it wasn't always about me. I had wanted to adopt one of the greyhounds that our local rescue agency sometimes brought to horse shows, but the time was never right. Eventually the right time arrived and Frazier, a very large brindle male came home with me. When we first met he was very quiet and shy. He asked only one question – "Are you taking me?" He was very obedient and well-mannered with the cats and horses, but it seemed to take forever for him to understand about names. He was strictly a kennel dog with very little connection to humans. For days he kept telling me his name was "Brindle Dog Number Seven." Obviously he had lived in kennel number seven. People were to be respected, but that was the end of his understanding of humans. Berrie loved Frazier and tried to play, but he refused and showed us that he had no concept of what playing with dogs or people meant. He seemed to enjoy riding in my truck, and began to accompany me on drives around the farm, staying close to me on a long leash while I watched my horses train. I was afraid he would run away if I took him off the lead because he didn't answer to a name, nor did he appear to have linked emotionally to Berrie or me. As he spent more time with us I could see his eyes soften, and noticed a brief response to his name and dog treats.

We were busy with horse shows, and Frazier joined Berrie as a horse show dog. He enjoyed the activity, adjusted to sleeping in motels and was content to stay by the tack room door while Berrie sat in her dog pen inside the tack room. I noticed some problems with his legs and back when he jumped in and out of my truck and took him to my vet to be examined before we left for several weeks of horse shows in North Carolina. The vet felt that the soreness was the result of several things. First, he was a very large dog, and we suspected that he had been given various drugs at the race track to build up body size and to keep him sound. After he left the track his body was adjusting to lack of medication and was showing some soreness. I agreed to bring him back when I returned from the horse show if I thought he was still having leg problems.

Frazier quickly fell into the pattern of the horse show life, and I felt confident enough to let him off his leash each afternoon when the show ended for the day. He joined other dogs in playing in the barn and really looked as if he was smiling all day long. He had also learned his name, and, with encouragement from our groom, Frazier started to jump in and out of the back of our truck when it was parked in front of the barn. After two days of playing, Frazier started to experience severe back problems. One night he woke up in the motel room crying in pain. He could stand up but was very unsteady on his legs. It took me what seemed an eternity to find an emergency clinic that could give me directions on how to find them. When I got

Frazier there he was completely paralyzed and had to be carried into the clinic. He had lived with me only a month and there was little I could tell the doctors about his past medical history. All the tests ruled out poison and countless other possibilities. After two days in the clinic he was still paralyzed. His diagnosis was a back injury, from the race track, that was now causing neurological problems. The sympathetic veterinarians gave me three options: they would operate with no guarantee of his ever walking, they would sedate him and let me drive him ten hours back to Kentucky, or we could put him to sleep. I could not rationalize surgery with more pain for a dog of his young age and size, so with much sadness I elected to euthanize him.

After I returned home I asked the Universe why such a wonderful dog had been in my life for such a short time. The answer really surprised me. Frazier had experienced many unhappy, abusive lives as a dog. He kept reincarnating to find and enjoy a happy life. Before he came to me he was well on his way to another unhappy life here. To give him the opportunity to experience joy, love, and caring humans he was sent to me. His short stay on the planet was not a lesson intended for me. It was strictly to allow him to experience the love and joy he had been searching for. I want to thank the Universe for sending Frazier, Joe Dog, Berrie, Morgan, and Mollie to me. These kind, understanding animals were present to help me through each part of my life. They joined with my horses to show me love and remind me that I was never alone.

CHAPTER 9

The Animal Communication Workshop

From the time that I presented my first animal communication workshops, I have tried to refine and develop a method of teaching what I call a new language. It is not a foreign language, because we are all born with this skill. The language of animals is both visual and telepathic, being composed of pictures and of the thoughts and feelings that we receive. All of us are born with these skills or abilities to communicate without words. As we grow up in a verbal world we bury our intuitive abilities. My job, as a teacher, is to give people the tools they need to reopen this part of themselves.

I wish to preface this chapter with several of my views on teaching nonverbal communication. First, I do not believe this is a skill that can be effectively learned by reading a book or watching an instructional video. I believe that a person has to be present, when first learning this new way to talk, with other people and animals. This new language consists of energy, or energy vibrations. It is a sensation you need to feel in your physical body. I can give directions and homework, but at the beginning I find it is more effective if another person or persons can confirm the feelings and pictures that you receive. I have attempted to teach this language on a one-on-one basis, but have found that it works better with groups of people. Again, I believe this has to do with the energy vibrations around us, and, in my experience, my students do learn faster in small groups.

Secondly, there is no right or wrong way to receive information from your pets. Many people get clear pictures, while others get intuitive feelings. This language varies for everyone. As you practice, the information or responses will generally become a combination of pictures, feelings and thoughts. Part of this has to do with the pets themselves. Some animals send more pictures, while others send feelings. It just depends on the animal you are talking to, and your level of communication skills.

Thirdly, this is a skill all of us possess at birth. As we become verbal it gets pushed down and covered up, but it never leaves us. At times, family members may shame us out of it by telling us that dogs and cats can't talk. As we are encouraged to develop verbal skills, our nonverbal communication or intuitive abilities tend to become buried and closed off. All you need to rediscover this ability is the belief that you can do it and the desire to work at it.

If you choose to learn this language you will find not only a closer relationship with your pet, but I hope you will also eventually come to recognize how all species on this planet are closely related. Of course you will learn more about your pet, but you will also begin to feel the Universal energy that enables us to feel energy from wild animals, and even plants and trees.

I prefer to conduct two-day workshops when I teach nonverbal communication. There are two reasons for this: first, just the actual experience of working with energy, or learning to send and receive mental images, can be physically exhausting for some people. Secondly, I want everyone to bring one of their pets – a dog, cat, bird, etc. – to the practice group that is held on the second day. The first day's session generally runs three to four hours, which is too long for most pets to sit and be quiet. It can become too distracting for the students to take care of their restless pets and learn nonverbal communication at the same time.

The workshop begins with a meditation, in which each person learns to visualize certain objects in their mind's eye. I use a very basic meditation, asking each person to visualize themselves in a beautiful grassy meadow. As they enter the meadow I ask them to place a lake, a tree and other objects wherever they wish. As they position each object I offer some guidance about colors, and what to feel, such as cool water or bright warm sunlight, as they enjoy this tranquil scene. As they build the picture they become the artist. Eventually, they add leaves to a tree, and finally add a beautiful rainbow to the sky. While they paint the rainbow in their mind's eye, I ask each person to feel the colors, and then to feel the qualities that each color represents. For example, spiritual sensations are associated with violet, healing with green, joy with yellow and so forth. I believe each person must have some experience in visualization to be able to construct their first sentences in the nonverbal language.

After this meditation ends I ask each person to breathe deeply and feel the joy and energy from the picture that they created in their mind's eye. This serves two purposes – I have helped to focus their concentration, and have hopefully removed some of the clutter and noise from their mind. The ability to shut out the clutter and slow your brain to reach a certain level of concentration is absolutely necessary to work with nonverbal communication. You must be open to receive the thoughts or images from the pets, and there is no way to do this with your mind full of thoughts about business, home, children, grocery shopping, and other distractions.

The other reason for this meditation is to let people practice composing a picture using their own visualization skills. As you will discover, in order to ask questions of the animals you must be able to picture them in some type of scene or place, and then let the animals fill in the empty spaces as they respond to your question. An example of this might be asking a dog if he likes to be inside or outside at his home. You ask this question by picturing him outside in an open space or yard. He will respond by sending you a picture with the blanks filled in – a fence of some type, the side of a house or trees if he spends time outside – or, if he is primarily an inside dog, you will usually receive pictures of the inside of a house. On a more advanced level, I might need to ask a show horse if he is more comfortable competing on an outside course or in an indoor arena. He will tell me his preference by sending back an image of jumping outside or in the indoor arena. If I get images of both an indoor and outside course, I know that he really doesn't have a favorite area to compete in.

The meditation is followed by a series of specific visualization exercises. I describe the mind or inner eye as a blank screen, like an empty movie screen. Next, each person is asked to visualize one single object, usually a ball of some type, such as a soccer ball, football or golf ball, and place it in the center of the screen. Once they can picture that ball, I add another ball of a different type – a golf ball added to the soccer ball – and tell them it is to be placed to the right or left of the first ball, keeping both in a straight line. Then I add one more ball – or an object of a different shape, like a golf club or tennis racket. This object also goes in the straight line: for example, I begin the exercise with a golf ball in the middle, add a soccer ball to the left and finish with a golf club on the right side of the golf ball. Now the object of the exercise is to maintain focus and hold the objects in a straight line. Once this has been achieved, I ask the students to move one object higher up on the screen, then move it either to the right or left side – in other words, to keep changing position of the objects while keeping them in clear focus on their mind screen.

The classes usually do well until I ask them to change the position of the objects on their screen. It takes intense concentration to move the objects without letting them go out of your focus. This exercise becomes one of my homework topics for the class. In order to form the sentences composed of visual images, you have to learn to send out certain simple pictures without losing the focus. Another example of this is asking a dog or horse who his dog or horse friends are. The sender must first picture the animal they are talking to, then send a general picture of him with other dogs or horses. Instantly, they will receive back a picture with different animals that their subject has added to the picture in order to answer the question. The animal will send pictures back of himself with specific companions. For horses, it may be pictures of gray or chestnut horses. For dogs, you might get a picture of a dog with long or short hair or a dog of a different color and shape, but it is necessary to send out some type of basic image of other animals to ask this question.

From this point I move on to actually forming sentences with visual images. Once someone has become comfortable with the visualization exercises they find this to be fairly easy. In forming sentences with visual images you must include pictures of many more objects. You must picture your animal doing specific things and send pictures of him in a specific place. An example of this more advanced communication would be helping a horse with problems he might have in the show ring. A horse might spend too much time looking at sights outside the ring or actually worry about jumping over a certain type of jump. In order to help him I would need to send pictures of him jumping each obstacle as well as sending him thoughts to keep him focused on his rider while he is in the ring. This level of communication is much more advanced than asking questions like, "What do you like to eat?" and "Who are your friends?" In more advanced communication the sentences include picturing the animal beginning and ending a specific task. For a horse, it may be jumping a course, or, for dogs, performing specific commands in a dog obedience class. A sentence, in visual images, must show the animal doing exactly what the owner or trainer wants. If you send out incomplete pictures you will confuse the animal. As I mentioned in an earlier chapter, it is also confusing if the owner keeps giving commands that include negative words while the visual pictures that the animal responds to send a different message. I explain that there is no picture among the visual images for negative words found in the spoken language. To work around the lack of negatives, you must send out images picturing the animal doing the specific (positive) behavior that you want. Animals do learn the meaning of negative words, but it is usually from our tone of voice or our behavior when they have done something incorrect. Being able to send the positive pictures also gives our animals a sense of security and confirmation that they read our minds correctly.

In staying with a positive outlook you must remember what I believe is one of the most important aspects of animal communication: just because we can send and receive pictures, we cannot always get the animal to do what we want. Nonverbal communication is no different than verbal communication with friends and family – just because we can talk to one another does not mean we can make them behave as we want them to. It is exactly the same way with animals – the ability to speak their language does not mean you have control of them. When I first read Beatrice Lydecker's book on animal communication I would ask my horses to walk up to me in the field. They would raise their heads, look at me, then go back to their friends. I was making contact, though I didn't realize it at the time, but they saw no reason to leave their friends and walk over to me. This new language gives us a deeper link or connection to our animals but it is not a form of control.

At first, it is always easier to send out a thought or message than to receive one. These thoughts or energy vibrations move in the blink of an eye. They are exchanged much faster than in spoken language. In receiving an image you may experience feelings as well as mental pictures. You may also get several equally correct answers to one question. For example, if you ask a dog where he likes to sleep you may get a human bed, his dog bed and a couch. The animals also show us that they can direct their answers to different people – one person may see a couch, another a dog bed. This is the time when you need someone with you to confirm the answers or responses.

After a workshop, I always suggest that friends try to practice together so that they can give each other confirmation of certain images. It is also much easier to talk with pets that you do not know. I have found that, at first, dogs and cats at home usually don't send out good clear pictures to their humans. They have already developed a form of communication through body language or habit and routine and don't see the need to send pictures. In addition, you already know most things about your pet, so it may be hard to decide whether you got an image from him, or if you just believed that was his answer. In my experience, it's always easier to start my students off by practicing talking with pets that they have never met. From the animals' side they are usually more open with people they don't know than with their own human family. I feel they are more open with strangers for several reasons. As I said before, your own pets have already established ways to talk to their owners and they seem to feel that there is no need for images when the owner already knows how they feel, or what they like and dislike. In some cases, they will send pictures but will shut off the images when the owner does not

70

acknowledge them. Also, many animals have made it clear to me that they want their privacy respected, meaning they do not want their owners to know everything they do or think. These cases range from the dog that likes to do something his owner thinks is inappropriate, like sleeping on the owner's bed when the dog is left alone, to the dog that feels his owner worries excessively about his health or happiness. Many people, in their efforts to be good owners, or those with great love and attachment for their pets, can annoy the pets with their constant worries. When the pets pick up these feelings, they become unsettled because the owner is worrying so much. Talking with a stranger is like meeting a new animal friend, and they respond fairly quickly with good images the same way they would talk with a new animal in their life.

The second day of a workshop is a time for me to answer questions, and for each student to practice with the animals attending the class. I limit my class size because I want each person and pet to receive as much attention as necessary. I have the class ask each pet some basic questions – for example, where do you sleep, what is a favorite food, or who are your animal friends. Then I ask the owners to confirm the answers, or elaborate if necessary on what the pets have said. I also ask the owners if they have a specific question for their pet. Usually the questions are as simple as, "Who is your favorite person?" However, with so many pets coming from animal rescue groups, many people want to know about the pet's life before it entered their family.

In presenting a workshop, I also include some of my own thoughts and personal views on living with and working with your dog, cat, horse, or other pet. Even though you can learn to speak your pet's language it does not mean you can get them to do specific things or change their personalities or completely rid them of an undesirable behavior. Learning to speak with them provides insight into why they do something or how they feel about certain things. Speaking their language becomes a training aid: understanding what upsets them is an aid in how to deal with problems or events. After receiving the information, it is up to the owner or trainer how to use this information to proceed in working or living with the animal.

You cannot change the basic instinct that your pets were born with. You need to respect their personalities and instincts and try to work with them. For example, in choosing a dog, try to consider what the dog was bred to do. Dogs bred to herd sheep or hunt rabbits may not be the best choice if you have limited time and space to exercise them. With horses, try to pick one whose breed fits with your goals. For example, Thoroughbreds with a racetrack past are probably not the best choice as a trail or pleasure horse. All animals are adaptable, but if you put some thought into what you expect of the animal you are bringing into your home the result may be the best possible match between pet and owner.

In my experience with animal communication it has been proven to me that the majority of our pets do not understand their sexual urges. These urges or feelings to which their body reacts are just a physical response to hormones. Please be responsible in any type of breeding. It has been my experience that most pets, whether they are dogs, cats, or horses, are happier if they do not have to deal with these urges that they don't fully understand.

Finally, always remember that you are the leader of the pack. Even though your dog or cat may tell me they would like another dog or cat friend to live with them, the ultimate responsibility is yours. If you feel that you have too much to cope with, use your own judgment before adding to your animal family. Remember that all animals need to be socialized and trained whether they are house pets or show dogs. Training helps them adjust to different situations, gives them security and links them to you, especially if you have made it clear what you expect of them. In working around horses, remember that they are bigger and heavier than their human caretakers. Please don't treat them like small animals, and make sure they learn to respect the space around your body and that you respect their space in return.

CHAPTER 10

Tools for the Pet Communicator

The most important tools for the pet communicator are: stop, look, listen and learn to feel. The ability to stop means stopping the clutter in your mind. After you tune out or stop hearing noise and can ignore visual distractions it is much easier to focus on communicating with your pet. It is necessary to listen to your pet and have a clear space in your mind to see the images that the animal sends you. When you can focus completely on the animal you begin to see images, feel your own intuitive feelings, and the feelings transmitted by your pet. The language for nonverbal communication translates into visual images and feelings. Unlike most new experiences, where seeing is believing, this language requires that you believe before you are able to see. A failure to believe you can receive images and feelings will effectively act as a block to your ability to do so. I confirm the visual images by the feelings and energy vibrations that enter my body. If I am unsure about the meaning of thoughts or images coming to me I wait to receive more feelings or images from the pet. When I receive confirmation, it may feel like cold chills or warm water rushing through me. These vibrations that confirm information for us will enter our bodies instantly, with no effort on our part. If I have read a thought or image incorrectly I have no energy vibrations entering my body.

The ability to look is not just seeing or receiving the images from your pet. It is the ability to slow down the images, put them in slow motion and then put them in replay whenever you need to. I cannot fully describe, with words, how quickly images are transmitted to us from the animals. In my readings I find it can be necessary to hold the images on my mind screen and look at them for more details. An example of this is viewing the visual images from a lost dog or cat. I might need to closely examine their view of a house to look for details on color, window size or shape or the number of trees in an area, in answer to my question, "show me where you are now?" If you feel that the information coming to you via the pictures is incorrect, stop and repeat your question and then see what images you receive. If you are receiving the same images and/or feelings, your first information was correct. When you slow down or replay the images you will pick up more details and receive more in-depth information from your pet.

The ability to listen does not relate to hearing the spoken word but to using your own intuition. Listening properly translates into confidence, the knowing that your first feeling, thought or visual image is the correct one when talking with the animals. Images come to us so quickly that people learning nonverbal communication often feel they have missed the pictures completely. The first flash of an image, or the first thought that comes to your mind is usually the correct one. If you only receive sections or parts of images, hold that first image on your mind screen, and ask the animal to send more images to you to complete the picture.

Learning to feel means the ability to understand what the pets feel physically, in their own bodies, as well as what they feel emotionally. In talking with pets we need to locate body areas that may hurt and we can learn to identify specific areas internally and externally that need attention. We can also use their physical feelings as a guide to some things they may need or want in their life. A dog that sends me the overwhelming feeling of great amounts of energy and excitement may benefit from more physical exercise with his owner. By the same token, a racehorse might send the feeling that he has the desire to race but feels that he needs more physical training before he races again. One of the strongest emotional feelings I receive is that of abandonment. I work with many owners whose pets have come from animal shelters and rescue agencies. These small animals always tell me if they were abandoned or actually lost and they also know if they were sent away because the previous owners could no longer keep them. Other emotional feelings may range from joy, when playing with their humans, or to sadness if a family member leaves home.

When you begin animal communication remember that the first step is to stay open to the images or feelings that are transmitted to you. Many people let their preconceived ideas about the animals interfere when they attempt to process the pet's visual images and feelings. In a workshop practice session I asked a horse if he enjoyed being ridden. He answered with pictures of himself in a Western saddle and bridle and the feeling that he enjoyed being ridden. It made him feel "special" and "important." However, his new owner told us that when she did ride him he acted very nervous and unsure, leading her to believe that he did not enjoy being ridden. When I asked the horse about this, he relayed pictures of being ridden bareback and the feeling that this owner was very unsure about how to ride either with or without a saddle. Her lack of experience made this horse nervous and he clearly sent me feelings that he was afraid she might fall off.

The second step in beginning animal communication is the ability to weave the visual images with the thoughts and feelings, both emotional and physical, that you receive from the animal. In order to speak the animals' language fluently you first need to receive images and feelings from them, and then learn to send them out in the same way. For example, if I am working with a dog afraid of thunderstorms I will repeat the word "safe," while picturing him in a specific room of his house. The word "safe" translates for the dog, into the feeling of security and safety if he remains in one particular place during the storm. Then I use the word "brave," which translates into a feeling of self-confidence for the dog, thus conveying to him in images and feelings that he is a brave dog and will be safe in a certain room until the storm ends.

I have learned to use many combinations of images and words to work with all animals. Once you have learned to receive their images and feelings you have the tools you need to develop your skill as an animal communicator.

CHAPTER 11

What Animals Want us to Know and What We Can Learn from Them

When I ask workshop participants what they feel they can learn from a pet, the number one answer is "unconditional love"; but I believe the next important things to learn are how to live in the moment and how to approach death. Yes, animals do show us unconditional love. They don't care if our grades are good in school; they don't care if we are short or tall, or fat or thin. Most animals that enter our lives want to have a job or serve a purpose, but some of them just want to be dogs and cats doing dog and cat things. For dogs, it's digging in the dirt, or going outside to run and play – while cats enjoy staying up at night and hunting, even if they have a life inside the house. A job for our pets may be as simple as guarding the house while we are away, or going on walks with their humans, while others feel that being a pet therapy dog or performing in obedience classes at dog shows is an important part of their life. For our dogs, having a job keeps them more in touch with their family and pack. On the other hand, my cats tell me that their jobs range from being a companion (all those head bumps and rubs) to being a great hunter, from chasing field mice to attacking bugs in the house.

Horses, however, are usually trained for a specific purpose, such as racing, showing, or being pleasure horses. At times they like to change jobs and try other things, but most of them consider their training to be the job that links them to humans.

The animals also want us to know that they choose to live with us in a furry or feathered body, and want to be respected for who they are. They really don't want to be little people. Although they want to do things with us, serve a purpose with us, they still want to be that dog, cat, bird, or horse that we took into our life. One of my favorite stories from the horse trainers I knew was their response to questions like, "Does that horse kick?" or, "Does he bite?" They would always reply, "He has teeth," or "he has four legs," meaning that in a certain situation you might be bitten or kicked – that's what horses do. Of course they would explain that the horse was well behaved, but you always had to live with the reality that they could bite or kick. The ability to acknowledge and understand each animal's instinct and purpose helps us respect them. Horses bred to race will want to run, and dogs that were bred to herd sheep or cattle will always have that herding instinct; they expect us to be aware of their personality traits. They do have specific instincts and they ask their humans to take time to understand these traits.

The majority of domestic animals that I talk with let me know that they want to have some job or purpose that connects them to their human family. Showing us how to live in the moment is one of their greatest gifts to us. In over twenty years of animal communication, I have never had a pet say "I should have done that differently." They accept what they did, and, yes, they do reason or think some things out before acting, but if one of their acts results in an unpleasant conclusion they handle it and move on. They don't go back and worry about what they should have done. As I mentioned earlier, watching my own cat fall from a high tree was my first example of seeing an animal live in the moment. I have read many dogs and cats that have been abused or abandoned. I usually pick up some things from the past, but on the whole many appear to recover emotionally by having the ability to live in the moment. If they live in the moment, fear is usually gone from their lives. Amazingly many of these abused pets do not hold grudges or blame. Some simply screen out what happens. For others, their personality may have changed from being outgoing to becoming shy and reserved. The ones that seem to make the best recovery focus on where they are and who they are living with when I talk with them. They don't judge, they just stay in the moment and go on with their lives.

Pets with cancer or other health-related issues always show me how they do their best to live in the moment. In conversations with me they tell me if certain medicines or treatments make their bodies feel better. Or they may tell me what part of their body has pain. They do not transmit fears of pain or death to me; the main focus of their thoughts is on what they are doing at that minute. In other words, they do not appear to worry about what might happen, they concentrate entirely on what is happening in the present.

The animals know that we never die, but only make a transition that results in changing shape and form. Animals retain memory of being in spirit before they came to live on earth. They are aware that they will return to spirit when they leave the cumbersome body they used here. One of the most rewarding things I do with animal communication is to translate to an owner how his animal wants to approach this time of transition. Some sick or aging pets naturally pick up on the owner's fears and sadness over their transition and try to stay in their body for as long as possible. Animals tell me they want to cross over with dignity but have few fears about the transition process. When the animals are ready to cross into spirit, there are always other animal spirits present to escort them to the next stage. I have seen one of my own cats, already in spirit, return to escort the spirit of my dog from his cancer-filled body. Sometimes the animal spirits make themselves known to me before the transition occurs, and in other cases they escort the departing spirit to me for a good-bye. What I hear from most species is usually the same. When they can no longer physically get up and move or run to protect themselves they start to think about leaving their body. This is an instinct that is in almost all animals – the ability to flee or run to protect themselves. Our small pets do trust us to look after them and assist them in moving when their bodies age, but they are usually not happy in this condition. The animals always tell me that they know there is no "death" and that they know they can come back and visit their human families without a body.

Without fail, all the animals let me know that they come here to enjoy life on this planet to the fullest. They stay in the moment and enjoy what they are doing at that time. I know that the animals choose to be here, to be with us. They are not here to learn lessons the way we humans are. They are here to enjoy all the experiences life on earth has for them; and, whether they live for one year or ten, it is those experiences and the quality of life that they have come here to enjoy.

CHAPTER 12

Animals In Spirit

When I was growing up I was able to see and feel the energy of animals in spirit the same way that I saw and felt the spirits of deceased people who had lived in our house. As my nonverbal communication skills increased, I realized that I was getting messages from animals in spirit. The appearances of deceased pets used to come as a complete surprise to me. I was not asking for them to appear, but they used my abilities to communicate as a way to make their presence known. When I started a reading I might see a dog, cat or horse appearing to me as though suspended in the air, or hovering, while images I received of the animals living on this plane appeared more solid and grounded. I start all my readings by asking for a pet's name, not a physical description. As the pet's image appears to me, I describe to the owner the pet I am seeing. In this way I confirm, to my satisfaction, a connection with the pet the owner wants me to talk with. Eventually I realized that the first pet I saw was not necessarily my intended subject. The first image normally comes from the pet that wants to talk the most or be first. It was not unusual, in multi-pet homes, for the most outgoing animal to express a desire to talk first, then to have its image appear to me. I soon discovered that pets in spirit would use me as a way to reconnect with their owners. As I described an image I might hear the owner say – "you just described my childhood dog!" Then they often told me that they felt intuitively that there was still a connection to the pet that had died. Most of the time these pets would confirm for their owners that they were still a part of the owner's life. They might tell me about watching the new puppy that had joined the household or show me that they still napped in a favorite place in the home. They were content to be around the owner whether they could be seen or not.

As my skills in communication developed I became aware that I could connect with deceased pets whenever I wanted to. I may not always be able to connect with each spirit an owner might wish to talk with. However, I will get, from my guides, some information about them. At times I am told that a specific spirit has reincarnated and is on this plane again. I will usually not be told where the pet is living or who they are with but I am told if they are on earth again. The majority of the pets will appear and tell me how they died and who they are with in spirit, either animals or humans or both.

As I have mentioned earlier, some lost animals I had been asked to look for would appear to me in pictures with beautiful, strong, bright colors around them. This was their way of letting me know they were in spirit. When I first started my animal readings none of my clients ever asked me if I could talk to a pet in spirit or Heaven. Now, as my clients' levels of awareness have grown, I get many calls to reach pets that have crossed over. The animals' activities in spirit appear to be unlimited, but at times they tell me that they have chosen specific jobs. They may be working in a hospital or healing center with adults or children who have crossed into spirit. Others act as guides for other animals that are crossing back to spirit, while some tell me they are caretakers of the spirits of young animals (like puppies or kittens) that transition at a young age. In other instances they show me where they live and play – which is usually a place with emerald green grass and clear sky. Sometimes they are with people, and sometimes with other animals. Many times they show me that they are back with a specific person or family member in Heaven. Others tell me about visiting their family on this plane and how easy it is to come back and be with their earth family after they have left the heavy body they occupied here.

There are also the pets that we have a difficult time releasing into spirit. They show me that they try to stay with their owner in their body until the owner feels ready for them to move on into spirit. On the other hand, it's not unusual for a pet to describe still being with his old family after he has left his body and moved into spirit. These pets have been fully released. They stay because they want to. In one reading, a woman asked me to contact her dog that had crossed into spirit. Her dog informed me that he was still with her, and showed me the inside of the apartment. He was just enjoying life and doing his job of being with his owner. At the end of the reading, the client confirmed that she could feel her dog brush her leg and that her downstairs neighbor would hear him thump down into his dog bed just the way he had done when the spirit was in his body.

Many years ago I was asked to look for a lost dog, but I was not called until the dog had been missing for three months. When pets have been gone that long I always ask for a photograph to make my connections easier as I try to reach the pet. The owner sent me a flyer showing the missing dog's picture. I remembered seeing this flyer on our grocery store bulletin board, and the feeling I had then of the dog being in spirit. When I tried to reach the dog, I got back very clear pictures of a farm where the dog appeared to be living. I was also shown two other dogs that the missing dog said she was with. When I related this to the owner, she confirmed the farm pictures but said the other dogs were not familiar to her. Each time I contacted the dog I got similar pictures – farm scenes and the other dogs. Eventually I realized that this dog was in spirit and that the other dogs were her companions or guides. The images from this dog were so clear that it was hard for me to realize at first that she had crossed over. However, none of the images that I received ever showed any people or any activities that the dog was engaged in. She appeared to be spending her time walking on a farm accompanied by her two dog friends. Eventually I concluded that the dog was in spirit, but she was not ready to sever all the ties with her human family. When the owner did discover the dog's body she was able to find some closure and release the spirit. Then the dog and her spirit friends went on.

In another reading, a woman asked me to contact her dog in spirit and ask when he would return to her and what breed of dog he would be. When I reached the dog, a cocker spaniel, he told me the usual things: that he was happy, was resting and enjoyed being out of a body that didn't feel good or move easily. His next pictures surprised me. I saw him sitting on a sofa, looking at a book with his owner. Then I saw a picture of a Welsh terrier. I told the owner that he would return as this breed and asked her about the dog looking at a book with her. She told me that they had had many talks about him returning to her, and that they looked at books of dog breeds to pick out a new body. She wanted me to confirm that the dog had understood her wish for him to return to her. She hoped he had decided on a Welsh terrier, because she wanted a small dog with a large dog spirit.

Another owner asked me to contact her dog in spirit just to see if she was all right. The dog immediately told me that she was happy and appreciated all her owner's efforts to keep them together as long as possible. In treating her dog's cancer the owner had changed veterinarians several times to try new treatments to prolong and improve the quality of her pet's last few years. Then I started to see pictures of balloons and a house, and asked the owner if she had recently had a party. She told me that when her dog did go into spirit she had a party, to release her spirit and celebrate her transition. She put balloons on her porch and on her yard gate, and each person invited shared a small remembrance of time spent with the departed pet. The dog told me that she was there for the party and loved the celebration.

At other times, the contact with our pet in spirit may just be in one of our dreams. People often tell me stories of a departed pet appearing in a dream just to let them know that everything is all right. Of these, the most memorable was a woman telling me about a dream where her cat swam a river to reach her, then swam back to the other side and disappeared. The owner said her cat always had a great dislike of water and she believed it meant that her cat had no fears and was happy on the other side.

As I worked with more pet owners I saw how comforted they were by knowing that their pets were happy with life on the other side. A large percentage of owners were not able to say good-bye to pets that had died in accidents, while others want to make sure that the pets understood why they were euthanized. I feel that talking with animals in spirit gives closure to the owners and in some instances confirms that their pets are still connecting with them from the other side.

The main thing I have learned from this part of my work is that death is just another transition. It is not an end, there is nothing final, our pets just move on to a different part of life the same way that we do. I am able to see the spirit of the pet being accompanied by animal guides after the pet's spirit leaves his body. These guides are not always animals the owner has known, but are guides that help the pet move from a life on earth back to life in spirit.

I know from talking to pets in spirit that they have free will and choices, just as humans do. They may choose to return to earth as the same species or they may pick a different life in a new body. A rabbit may decide to return as a house cat, or the house cat may choose to be a mountain lion. In any event, there are no limitations and the choices seem endless.

In all my talks with animals living in spirit, the most overwhelming feeling and thought I receive from them is the feeling of safety. All the species convey by images and thoughts that they are living in a place of harmony and tranquility. They all feel safe, there are no predators and they have no fears.

CHAPTER 13

When Our Animals Reincarnate With Us

The concept of our animals returning to be with us again and again was always easy for me to accept. In growing up I had always felt closer and more connected to my animals than I did to most of the people in my life.

I believe that at times certain animals do come back to help us achieve some goal or accomplish a specific lesson that we need to learn in this lifetime. In other cases, I think we reunite to share each other's love and joy of being on earth together.

One of my paint horses, now in spirit, appears in the dreams of his groom, Kathy, who loved and cared for him on my farm. She tells me he appears as an Indian war pony – with feathers in his mane and war paint on his face. I take this to mean that he feels free to be the spirit horse he wanted to be. When he contacts me, he says life is grand and he tells me who his horse friends are in spirit – but he apparently gives Kathy the picture of a favorite horse life.

In my own life I have had several specific instances of animals returning to me. The first instance of this reuniting was with my horse Bold Paddy. He made it clear, when he lived with me, that we did know each other long before I was ready to acknowledge this part of our relationship. When I began my past life regressions, there was Paddy, his energy and eyes completely familiar and recognizable to me in the same way that I had been able to recognize different people in my other past life regressions. The first time I saw him in a regression, I was working on a relationship issue with a man in this lifetime. I had never thought to ask about my animals in past lives because I was concentrating on how to deal with people in my current life. At the start of the regression I asked my guides to give me insight into past issues with this particular man. I was led to a frontier life where both of us were young men and apparently good friends. Once again I was working with horses – a familiar past life theme for me – and was employed as a wagon driver. Paddy was my best wagon horse. He was in a bigger, heavier body, but still a chestnut color and quickly recognizable to me through his eyes. Eventually, from information given to me in the regression, I saw that my friend was jealous of me in that lifetime and these issues were carried over into this life; but the main lesson for me in this regression was to confirm my past times with this horse, and to realize that we did know each other on many levels.

In the same series of regressions one of my paint horses, San Rosanna, made several appearances. She appeared as a paint horse – in my care, but not necessarily my own horse – in several Native American lives. I never felt that there were any lessons for her to help me with. I just received the strong feeling that we loved each other, trusted each other and enjoyed being together.

The most recent horse that returned to share this life with me was a Grand Prix show jumper named Jerry. The first time I saw him in the show ring I felt the instant recognition and attraction that I experience with certain horses. At the time it didn't occur to me that we had been together in any past lives. My business partner and I were putting together a new show horse stable, and we purchased Jerry as a Grand Prix horse for our business. Jerry instantly fit into our barn and he soon began telling me how high he could jump and how much he wanted to win in competition. Jerry did prove to be an over-achiever and a perfectionist in the horse world. His overwhelming desire not to make a mistake, like knocking a rail down, always resulted in him having an anxiety attack halfway around a jumper course. He would jump the first half of the course with no faults, then become anxious to finish. Wanting to pick up speed, he knocked down rails as he fought with his rider over his pace and approaches to the last jumps. In my talks with him, I tried to get some insight into his frustrations and unhappiness with the riders we had been using. To my surprise, he started to tell me how frustrated he was with me because I had not acknowledged or recognized our personal past life connections. When I asked him for more details, he showed me oceans, deep water, and swimming effortlessly together when we were dolphins. In my early past life regressions I had been told that I had been a dolphin at one time, but had completely forgotten this. Jerry also showed me another life when we were human lovers. I had always believed it was possible to change species but this horse was convincing me. Unfortunately I had to tell him that this time around he was the horse, I was his trainer and that it was time for us to have more new experiences, not worry about our past lives together.

My experiences with Jerry not only proved to me past life connections, but showed me that our animals are not always the pure, undamaged spirits or souls we expect them to be. I believe that his energy or spirit wanted to experience life on many levels while using different bodies to explore. I have had other animals explain fears in this lifetime by telling me about deaths or injuries that occurred in their past lives. For example, cats that are fearful and shy now often tell me about past lives as small animals that humans hunted for food.

My Scottish terrier Berrie, and my cat Mollie, who presently share my life, always tell me about our past lives. Mollie delights in talking about Egypt, telling me what I did as a healer there and how she was revered in her Egyptian cat lives. Berrie acknowledges past lives of companionship and fun. In her infinite wisdom she once told another psychic that she always incarnated to wealthy families because she enjoyed living on estates. She has recognized one of my friends as a past life sister of mine, telling us how she slept in our bed with us and saved us from a house fire when my friend and I were children. At this point in my life I don't need any more proof of my past life experiences, but I love it when the animals start to tell me about places we have been and things we have done before.

I currently have a client whose cat was formerly a Tibetan monk, and a friend whose retired champion show horse was her Indian war pony. One of my most touching past life readings came while I was doing a day of pet readings at a client's home. A man came with his dog, which he had found on his job construction site. This dog, several years old at the time, just appeared at the area where he was working. He adopted her and eventually brought her to me for a reading. She gave me little or no information on who her past owners were, or how she became lost or abandoned – just the basic information that she was always this man's dog. As I related the information, he began to tell me about his dog who had crossed into spirit, and a promise he had made to her that he would wait for her return. He had come to me in the hope that I would confirm that this was his dog and that she had returned again. She confirmed that she was the same dog by sending images of her previous body color and size.

I really believe that our pets return to us to give us joy, love and companionship. Some are natural healers using their love to help us with the rough spots in our lives. They come to love us and help us more fully expand and experience our lives here.

CHAPTER 14

Talking to Wild Animals

When you learn nonverbal communication you can talk not only with pets, but also with all animals and birds. Animals that live in the wild connect with us on various levels.

When you send out a picture, they will usually return your image with their own image, feeling, or thought. On the whole, the first feeling that comes to me from them is their amazement that I spoke the way they did – by using images. The next feeling is generally one that asks me not to harm them. I have seldom induced birds or animals to stay around long enough to have much of a conversation. For several years I had a deer who would stop by my house in the late afternoon. I would see her jump into a horse paddock by my kitchen window, then turn her head to see if I was around to talk to her. She felt safe by the house and I always believed that she came to feel my energy and to see if I was still talking to the animals. No matter how safe she felt I could not get her to stay for more than five or ten minutes. She spent most of the time asking me questions: Who was I? Was I a human? Who else lived in my house? She seemed to enjoy the brief time she spent with me, but her instinct always kept her very aware and ready to run at any moment.

The last animal communication workshop held on my farm in Kentucky introduced my students to talking with wild birds. This workshop was attended by a mockingbird. He spent several hours attempting to get my attention by chattering away while I talked. Finally one of my students insisted that I stop the class and talk with the bird. His message for me came from all the wild animals on my farm. Essentially he was their spokesman, and they had questions about who was buying my farm. Would the new owners respect all of the animals and birds, and let them live their lives there without harm? The birds and animals were so conscious of how I related to them that they felt safe on land that I cared for. I told him that I appreciated the feelings of the wildlife and hoped that the new owners would respect their safety. This mockingbird attended both days of the workshop, remaining perched in a tree above my class to allow the students to talk with him. He sent images to us of flying in the sky, of flying with other birds and of his life on the farm.

When I meet snakes they usually present me with territorial issues. They feel that I am intruding in a place that is theirs, not mine. When I promise not to hurt them they move on and so do I.

The insects – flies, bees, etc., will also talk with you. They are very curious about humans and they generally tell me they are attracted to us by certain scents or smells. From them I receive feelings that they have the right to share our space whether they are inside our houses or outside. Communicating with insects is very different from working with animals, birds or reptiles. The insects respond more on a level of group thought than of individual thought. When I communicate with them, the first thought is directed to their leader. I say silently that I wish to connect to the one or ones who are in charge. After that I send the next thought, sometimes asking what they want and then asking them to move to a new place. In my own home I generally explain to flies or bees that they are in my space and asking them to move to another space usually results in their moving on.

All of these animals, large and small, birds and reptiles, really send me the message of live and let live. They want to go on with their own lives, hunting, traveling or doing whatever their instinct directs them to do.

It is possible to communicate with all of them, but I feel their responses are based on how much contact they have had with humans. If they have not seen many people they will acknowledge our pictures by momentarily stopping their movement, or at least slowing down for a few seconds. These animals receive and process the images we are sending and they make some effort to evaluate how safe they are, before deciding how close to get or what type of conversation to have with us. We have to realize that they have a strong instinct that tells them to run from us, so any slowing down of their physical movement shows me that they received the image being sent to them. Animals that have had some contact with people will usually get a little closer before they turn and move away. It is as if they keep looking back over their shoulder to see how safe they are with us.

On a trip to Colorado I stopped to visit the Royal Gorge area. In the parking lot were two young deer with their antlers just starting to grow. The park employees kept trying to chase the deer away from the cars but they would return to take handouts of food from the tourists. They would walk within several feet of a tourist, check for food, then stretch their necks to take whatever food was offered to them. I saw them rubbing their heads on each other's backs and realized that their faces were itching – especially at the base of the antlers. I sent out a picture of me scratching their faces and one of them answered by coming close to me, then extending his head for a scratch. He was thrilled that I could provide such a service and we posed for pictures while I rubbed his head. The other deer kept a polite watch from several feet away but wouldn't come close to me. Eventually they moved off into the park and left the tourists. These deer had obviously been around people because they were able to interact on a certain level, but still listened to their instinct and were always ready to run if they felt the need to.

I have read several dogs that were half wolf and one that was half coyote. Each of these dogs had an energy completely different from a domestic dog. The wolf dog lived in a home with his human family and another wolf dog cross. They gave me a sense of wanting to be outside, sending me pictures of trees and sky coupled with a strong hunting instinct. They had a link or connection to their humans, but I received a feeling that being outside and hunting was the most important thing to them. The coyote/dog was very loyal and protective to her owner. She was very uncomfortable with other people and would pace excessively through the house, letting me know that something was missing or incomplete in her life. The images I received from her were never clear or well focused and I did not feel that she put any effort into returning my pictures. With this dog I got a sense that she could not focus her thought for more than a few seconds. She was not able to concentrate or follow the type of thought process that I had found in other dogs. The overwhelming feelings that came from her were of something missing her life. She was never content or at ease: while the wolf dogs knew what they wanted, the coyote dog stayed restless and unsettled each time I talked to her.

Living on my farm in Kentucky brought experiences with skunks and raccoons. As I have mentioned before, I practiced free feeding of my barn cats, and this habit encouraged skunks and raccoons to move into my horse barns. These animals would wait until late evening or early morning to sneak into the barns and help themselves to dry cat food. I returned to the barns between ten and twelve o'clock each night. If a skunk or raccoon was eating I would send out a picture of them eating while I filled the horses' water buckets or walked down the barn driveway. Eventually the raccoons and skunks would turn their heads and watch me but they felt safe enough to continue eating.

One raccoon showed me very clearly that she had become a close friend with the barn cats and wanted to move with them from my old farm to the new one in Paris. I had been putting food in pet carriers, which I had placed in the barn so the barn cats would become accustomed to the carriers before we moved. I had been sending pictures to the cats of me picking them up and placing them in the carriers. Each morning when I entered the barn to feed the horses I would find the same raccoon sleeping in a pet carrier. She kept returning pictures to me of her eating with the cats and a picture of her in a pet carrier that was being moved or picked up. I kept telling her with words and pictures that she was to stay on the old farm. When we did move the barn cats she sat in the barn loft and watched me move her cat friends to their new farm.

When I encountered the skunks I sent them the word "safe," along with images of them eating. I always hoped pictures of them eating would translate as the thought that I had no intention to harm them or interrupt their meal. I was always confident that they trusted me not to harm them.

It is fun to receive recognition from the birds and animals as they acknowledge our common language. The ability to communicate with them reinforces how interrelated we are. For me it is a wonderful feeling to know that all of us can share a common language.

CHAPTER 15

Looking for Lost or Stolen Pets

The search for lost or stolen pets can either be very rewarding or very frustrating. When a pet is lost it is important to start your search immediately. Place ads in the newspapers, put flyers on your street and on streets in nearby neighborhoods. There are many people who are interested and will try to help return lost pets to their homes. Make sure a tag is on the dog or cat's collar with the name of the owner (or pet's name) and a current telephone number. I have rescued dogs that were wearing collars with no identification tags or had tags with outdated telephone numbers. Start your search immediately. Don't wait to see if your dog or cat can find their way home. While you are waiting pets can become hopelessly lost, or even injured, so that they cannot return.

Helping owners find lost pets is part of my work as an animal communicator. As I mentioned in Chapter 3, my skills allow me to see and feel a geographical area that the dog is in, plus a direction – north, for example – that your pet has taken. What I see is essentially what your pet sees. I see everything at their eye level. I try to listen or pick up a feeling of cars, either heavy traffic or little traffic. I also pick up feelings about the types of buildings – if they are close together, like houses, or large buildings like a business or shopping area. One of the main things that I see and feel around the animal is water. This may consist of a small creek or stream, a river, or just mud puddles. It is also important to feel or look for how many people are in the area around the pet. I will usually feel if the pets are watching people or if they are in a more remote area where they seldom see or hear people.

Pet owners must understand that I can only give clues about where the pets are. The owners have to do the actual work in looking for the pets. I am not able to read street signs or house numbers because your pet cannot do that. Through years of looking for lost pets I have been able to combine information that comes in to me psychically with images from the lost pets themselves to pinpoint a specific location. My psychic abilities let me expand on what the pets are seeing. I will get more details, like the size, color and shape of buildings that are more complete than the images coming from the pet. What the pet sees generally comes to me as a picture of a building from the ground level, up to two or three feet high, since they don't see the whole building. At times I will sense psychically letters or numbers, either on a street sign or on a building, but I never really get a complete name or series of numbers. I can also sense fairly accurately how far and in what direction the pets may have traveled. Pets go farther than their owners think they possibly can. For example, many dogs following a trail with their nose tell me that when they stopped they had no idea where they were or how they had arrived there. These dogs were so intent on hunting that they failed to look up or look around to see any landmarks that could guide them home. At times dogs do seem able to follow a familiar scent or trail to return home.

However, very few dogs return by following their old trail. The majority of them tell me that they become disoriented and do not search for a scent.

In my personal experience, most lost animals do not have that wonderful, built in homing instinct or sense of direction that we see in movies about lost pets. The dogs and cats that travel great distances to return home need an enormously strong desire, and must have a finely-tuned sense of direction to find their way. I believe that domesticating our pets has resulted in their losing some of their intuitive or natural senses – the senses that enabled their ancestors to roam freely and return to the same places time after time. Our pets are totally dependent on us for so many things that I don't feel many of them are aware of an internal compass or guide that might return them to their home. My dog Joe was lost close to his home, but he had no idea of direction or how to return.

As I mentioned before, the pets' attitude about being in the world on their own plays a large part in returning them to us. There will always be animals that look at the world as one big adventure and really don't care if they get home. Others miss the familiar surroundings of a house and family, and will make every effort possible to come home.

The fact that animals live in the moment also plays a big part in what happens when they are lost. By staying in the moment they concentrate on eating, being safe by hiding, and protecting themselves. Because of this they are not putting energy or thoughts into where home is and how they are going to get back. Some of them may go up to a house or approach strangers in an effort to find a home. These pets feel that any home is satisfactory, and are so trusting that they take the risk, in the hope of finding a home.

When I read a dog or cat that has been lost, then rescued and placed in a new home, I get varying information about their homes. It is not unusual for the images they send to be out of chronological order in the animal's life. When I ask the pet for pictures of "your home or humans" I never know if I am receiving pictures of a home they were in before, or the home that they are presently in. I always have to ask the owners for confirmation on the pictures I receive.

When I first started to work with lost pets, I could not understand why the images didn't follow a chronological order or a time frame. As I gained more experience, I saw that the animals did not relate to time in the same way we did. They could always send me feelings of "young" or "old" for ages of themselves or others, but actual time frames, as we understand them, just didn't exist for them. I might receive the feeling of a long time, as in a long or a short number of days, but not much else came through in a time frame that we would call linear. Eventually I realized that charting time to put events in an orderly sequence simply didn't matter to them.

The first example of this came with a stolen dog that I was looking for. I had been able to make contact easily with her and had talked with her on several occasions during the first weeks I searched for her. At first, I only received pictures of a warehouse and a chainlink fence that stretched down one side of this building. Her owners had no success in finding the warehouse, even though the area

I directed them to had rows and rows of commercial as well as abandoned buildings like the one I had described. At one point I put the question in a different form. I asked her, "show me pictures of your house," rather than "show me where you are living now." I had already determined that this dog was kept at the warehouse, but I hoped she might get to leave and spend some time in a real house too. Instantly, I received images of a house close to water. I saw sand, a rustic wood home and strong water. Then I saw parts of the rooms from an inside view. When I called the owner with my new information he said I had just described his former home – one where he and the dog spent several years together. This dog knew the difference between a home with her owner and where she was currently living. Strangely enough, the dog sent few pictures to me of the house she was sharing with her owner at the time she was stolen. Almost all of her home images were of the beach house she liked. From this point on, I always confirmed each image with the owners before I come to a definite conclusion about where the animal was. Unfortunately, I was not able to reunite this dog with her family. Over the following months the only pictures I received from her were the same ones of a warehouse. Her owners continued to search, but she was never found.

When I attended one of Beatrice Lydecker's workshops, a cat showed us images of a house and a window ledge. It seemed that his first owners let him have the run of the neighborhood. When he returned home he jumped up on the window ledge and waited to be let in. The cat showed us that on one of his jaunts through the neighborhood he became confused and picked the wrong house. These people let him in the window, but they kept him, thinking he was a homeless cat. The cat was fairly unconcerned about his sudden change in homes and owners. He showed us images of the outside of similar houses and let us know in feelings that he thought at first he had returned to his original home. His new owners felt he was safer as an inside cat and did not let him go outside, so there was no way that he could have reached his old house. The new owners, who were taking part in the workshop, had run ads for a found cat but he was not claimed. This cat did not seem to have a preference of the homes. He stayed in the moment and adjusted to living with a new family. At the time it astounded me how quickly the cat had adapted and that he was emotionally unscarred by this event. As time went on, I came to realize that living in the moment was a normal reality for all the animals I talked with. It allowed lost dogs and cats to move easily from one home to another with minimal emotional baggage. We, as humans, place our own thoughts and emotions on our furry friends, but their view of the world is very different from ours. The stolen dog adapted to life with her captor and the lost cat adapted to a new house and family. I never felt the dog was totally at ease in her new situation, but her job was to adapt and she did. The cat basically told us that one home was as good as the other and that living in and for the moment was his main job.

I have been able to reunite many owners with their pets, but there are also a large number that never make it back to their original home. The ones that do are usually helped by kind people who find them and help them return. These are the people that take them in or respond to the "lost" ads and flyers that the owners put out. Many cats that are allowed to roam outside their homes become trapped in garages, basements, or unused buildings. At times these cats are found and returned to their owners, or they eventually find a way out and return home. One lost cat told me that she was closed up in what looked to me like a backyard storage shed. She had to look up to see a window and to me it looked as if there was wire on the inside of the window. This cat was actually very close to home, in a neighbor's garage. While the neighbors were out of town, the boy in charge of mowing the yard left the garage door open. The cat went in and was still there when the lawn mower was returned and the door locked. Several days later when the neighbors came home they found the cat, matched her with the flyers and called the owners. The owner called to tell me her cat was home and confirmed my pictures by describing the inside of the building, including an old cage sitting on a shelf in front of the only window. When the cat looked up from the floor, it looked as if wire covered the window.

In another reading, a cat showed me images of squeezing sideways between a door that slid open and a wall. She found her way into this unused warehouse while roaming on a hunting trip. However, when she got ready to leave she couldn't slide out by pushing on the door and was trapped for several weeks. When I asked her how she escaped she sent me pictures of a window. The window was made in two parts and apparently had to be cranked open or opened by a lever. She pushed on the upper section of the window and opened it enough to squeeze her body through the narrow opening. In the process of escaping she scraped the fur, in equal lengths, from each side of her body. Her owner confirmed for me that she returned with exactly corresponding scrape marks.

Sadly, not all lost cats return safely. I have also read for many who crossed into spirit because they became trapped in a basement or building where they could not escape and no one found them.

In the last few years I have helped find two dogs under what I feel were amazing circumstances. The first dog was the victim of a car accident. He was traveling in downtown Cincinnati to a dog show when his owner's car was struck by another car running a red light. The dog was not riding in a crate, but was sitting in the car's back seat. In the aftermath of the accident he escaped in the downtown area of this large city. From this point on he seemed to have vanished. When his owner called me I saw and felt the dog close to the river and under several bridges. He was scared and disoriented, and ran from any people who came close to him. The owner was able to find the area where I felt the dog was and people confirmed that they had seen him. However, he continued to run from everyone he saw, including his owner. After several weeks, in desperation, she took friends with her, hoping to be able to corner or trap him if they saw him. They were able to find him but he again ran in fright. When his owner yelled his obedience commands of "down, stay," he obeyed and remained down until she could reach him and attach a leash to his collar. I use this story to show people that no matter how close we are to our pets, they usually focus on their own safety; that their instincts and desire to be safe can be a hindrance to them returning to us. When our pets are on their own their instincts of running and hiding will generally prevail, making it harder to find and return them to their homes.

The other dog was stolen from her yard. (In most cases of stolen pets, the theft seems to be an act of impulse. I have only searched for two stolen dogs where I felt the theft was planned. In both instances, the dog was stolen because the thief held a grudge against the dog's owner and neither of the dogs was returned.) This stolen dog was an older one who recently had surgery. She had squeezed through a hole in her backyard fence and was standing in the next door neighbor's yard when a man driving down the street stopped his truck, got out and picked her up. When I was called, I felt strongly that the dog was taken in the hope of receiving a reward, or that the thief just wanted a dog like the one he picked up. I urged the owners to offer a reward on the flyers they put up as well as in their newspaper ads. The owners also emphasized in the ads that the dog had recently had surgery, needed special care, and that she belonged to some very unhappy children. The images I received from the dog were of the man who had her in his truck, with very few pictures of where she was at the time. In my next reading I saw what appeared to be kennels or cages like an animal shelter or veterinarian hospital. I was also able to give them a direction, east, and the fact that I felt the dog was fairly close to her home. The owner was afraid that the images were just those of the veterinary hospital where the dog had recently been, but when she checked the closest animal shelter the next day she found her dog.

She had been turned in by the man who stole her. He said he found her many miles from her home on busy highway and picked her up. I felt the flyers listing the dog's medical problems were a major factor in getting him to take her to the shelter. Stealing her had been an impulse, but at least the thief had enough compassion to return her to a place where she could be cared for.

I can generally give owners descriptions of areas where the pets are, or have been, as well as a direction and an idea of how many miles from home the pet is. It is hard to find them because of the limited scope of what they see around them, and because their own instinct to stay safe by hiding or running hinders the search. If they are not found in several days or weeks the images that come to me become weaker and it seems as if they stop trying to talk to me. If they have been found and are in a home the images usually stay fairly clear and seem to reach me easily. The animals on their own turn all their energy and attention to staying safe and caring for themselves rather than communicating with me. I know that the longer they are on their own my chances of finding them steadily decrease.

I usually know if the pet dies while I am searching for them. Most often the transition is confirmed when I receive an image of them in spirit. They are always in a young, healthy body and the colors around them are vibrant and shining. The images from spirit generally focus on the head and midsection of the animal, and I seldom see their feet. They seem lighter and not grounded, so the feet don't appear to be important. If a pet has crossed into spirit, most pet owners seem to have sensed the change before I confirm it.

I have been successful, in many instances, in reuniting pets with their families. Regrettably, there have also been cases when I was not able to help the pets return home.

CHAPTER 16

Benefits of Learning to Talk with Animals

One of the most rewarding aspects of my work is meeting the wonderful animals that come into my life. I love having the opportunity to tell people what their particular pet thinks and feels about his humans, his home and his life in general. When I start talking with the owners I share all the things our pets can teach us. Learning from the animals how to stay in the moment allows us, as humans, to enjoy what we are doing at that instant. Staying in the moment allows us to let go of our fears and concerns about past problems and what we perceive to be future problems. It gives us the opportunity to relax, learn to move with the energy around us, and enjoy life without fears. Being in the moment allows us to experience happiness and joy. We can take pleasure in the small things around us and be happy with the moment.

Learning to communicate the way your pets do establishes a close bond with them. It will not enable you to control them, but they will generally become more attentive and more aware of what you want them to do; or, at least, expect them to do. In some cases, speaking their language gives the animals more respect for us. At one workshop, a beautiful macaw attended the practice session. I saved talking with him until the end of the class and let the students start to practice with the dogs and cats. While we talked, by images, with the pets, the bird stayed fairly silent. I knew he felt he was far superior in intellect to the dogs and cats and I hoped that he would enjoy waiting while I worked with the students and their pets. When his turn arrived and the group started asking questions by sending pictures to him, he conveyed to me by his thoughts: "They're not stupid after all!" He loved the experience of a group sending images to him and he carefully returned feelings and images to us. He showed us the views from the windows in his home. We saw the dogs he lived with and received his feelings that they were too noisy.

Many clients tell me that their pets are more attentive and focused on them after a reading. And I know that any effort on the owners' part to send pictures makes their pets pay closer attention to them.

This form of communication will increase your levels of awareness about animals, nature, and the earth. When you can communicate with the animals, you are not limited: you are able to talk with wild animals, birds and an endless number of beings all around us. The flowers and plants in your garden communicate, as do the insects and creatures that live there. All you have to do is stay open to the possibility and believe that you can talk with them. When you accept this form of communication you accept a higher level of understanding and caring for all the life forms around us. I have always found it comforting to know that all of us speak the same language and that I am never alone; the animals, birds or plants are always available to talk with me.

After talking with so many animals, I know that they do not judge. They will always have likes and dislikes, but they do not judge people by race, size, or levels of education. They have a different set of guidelines, based on their instinct, to use when making friends.

I have found that learning to communicate with animals gives us a greater sense of security. It convinces me that there are no accidents, that each living form was placed here for a reason and that all of us are part of one great Creator's plan.

CHAPTER 17
Health Questions

When I started working as an animal communicator, questions from owners about health-related problems always formed a large part of the reading. The animals can tell me how they feel physically or how specific areas of their body feel. At first, the information about physical problems just seemed to pop into my mind. As I progressed in learning to speak nonverbally I developed a method of teaching my students how to uncover physical problems in the animals they talked to. In my workshop I refer to this as "Body Scanning." Body scanning information comes to me in several ways – in pictures, in intuitive feelings and in information from the animal itself. If I am actually present with the animal, I can also feel energy changes in various parts of their body.

When I first did body scanning I was always present with the animal. I was able to run my hands over a horse or dog's body and feel intensified heat in an area that might be sore or injured. I did not actually touch the body, but used both hands, palms down and held them about six inches from the animal's body. I started at the head and would move to the neck, to front legs, to the midsection and finish with the back legs and hindquarters. When I started I always allowed my hands to move freely, returning and repeating my hand movements when I was intuitively drawn to a specific area of the body. Feeling energy in this way proved to be fairly accurate, but because it took time to do and required me to be present with the animal, I started to develop what I feel is a quicker and more accurate way to check for physical problems. I reasoned that if I could receive images from the animal's mind I should be able to receive images or locate problems in the body in a similar fashion. Now I focus my attention and put all my thoughts and energy on quickly scanning the body. I start at the pet's head and go down the body with my eyes, using my eyes the same way I used my hands. If I am doing a phone consultation I already have a clear mental picture of the animal I am working with, so I hold the image of that pet's body on my mind screen and begin to check for health problems. I see things in the animal's body and can also sense if there is a problem. A sore throat will actually look red and irritated. If it is healthy it will be a soft pink color. If I am working with a racehorse who has choked in a race I will be able to see his lungs filling with blood and feel a sensation of not being able to breathe. If cancer is present I generally see tumors as red or inflamed color splotches. The larger the colored area the more the cancer is spreading. If a tumor is benign the area will look white and fatty with no red areas. Organs that are not functioning properly, like the liver, kidneys, heart, and lungs, will appear to have no energy or movement in them. If they are normal they have a flow of energy in and around them. Liver or kidney failure may also be sensed as a feeling of a blockage or tightness in that area of the animal's body.

If there are digestive problems I tend to receive a feeling rather than seeing a color in that section of the body. These problems come to me as a feeling of discomfort that can translate to our own bodies' feelings of indigestion.

I can usually tell if eye problems are present when a reading starts. The images from an animal with cataracts or vision loss will be blurry, with less color, and will lack sharp clear focus. At times the animals tell me themselves that their eyes have problems.

I am generally alerted to ear infections by the animals. They tell me if there is a problem with itching, soreness or pain in their ears. Teeth problems are also transmitted to me in feelings by the animal. They tell me which tooth or what area of their mouth may be sensitive.

In an animal with strained or injured muscles, the energy in that area is more intense and I am drawn to the leg or area of the back that is sore or stiff. When the animals describe these aches and pains it comes to me as a feeling of weakness in a specific area rather than pain. Broken bones come as feelings of pain in addition to a weakness when animals convey to me that their body is not functioning or moving properly. Arthritis is always a feeling of stiffness with some discomfort rather than sharp pains. I am constantly surprised at the large number of older dogs who seem to develop arthritis in their feet before other joints become affected.

I sense allergies as feelings rather than as anything I see in the body. Some animals tell me that their eyes are watery or that they have been sneezing when I consult with them. Others will tell me

117

about their skin feeling dry, irritated or even hot. Food allergies or sensitivity to specific foods come to me as intuitive feelings rather than anything I see in a body scan or from information that comes from the animal.

Horses tell me their front legs and hooves are the areas of most stress and discomfort. A body scan will quickly take me to sore feet, loose shoes or inadequate blacksmith work. Even if the horse has recovered from foot problems he will tell me about a foot injury or poor blacksmith work. I feel, intuitively, the jarring or stress on their front legs while they are being ridden and trained. Almost all the horses in training experience these physical sensations to varying degrees, and quickly tell me how good it feels to have cold water, liniment or ultrasound treatments applied to their legs or other parts of their body.

At times the animals have alerted me to future health problems while I was consulting with them. A Corgi dog came for a reading on his neck and back injuries and then told me about pain in a front paw. His veterinarian examined the paw and found a small cancerous tumor. Several racehorses have told me of a weakness or sore spot on a front leg, which unfortunately developed into more serious injuries as their training progressed.

I cannot always tell, from what animals say to me, how sick they might be. In my experience they know that parts of their bodies do not feel right or move easily but often they do not seem to be aware of how sick they are. Animals with cancer may tell me they have pain in one area but they never say "I have cancer," or another disease. They do not know our terms for disease. They are aware that their energy levels decrease and they tell me that they are tired, or can't play as much as they would like to or move as quickly as they once did. They make me aware of changes in their body after specific veterinary or therapeutic treatments. They convey feelings of an upset stomach from medicines they are given or tell me how good their body feels after ultrasound or chiropractic treatments.

In doing consultations on the health of an animal I hope to alert the owner to potential problems and give them information that comes to me from the pet. I hope the information on how animals feel physically will aid the owner in working with their veterinarian or health care professional. I do not do animal healing, but use my skills as a communicator to direct owners to healers they can work with. These healers may be veterinarians, either traditional or holistic, massage therapists, acupuncturists, or chiropractors.

CHAPTER 18

Most-Asked Questions

In my career as an animal communicator I have seen a very noticeable change in the questions owners want me to ask their pets. When I first started to do readings, the first questions were generally about behavior issues. "Why does my dog do that?" "Why won't he listen to me?" These would be followed by health-related questions such as, "How badly does his back (or leg, or neck) hurt?"

However, in the last few years the most often-asked question has been, "Is my pet happy?" "What can I do to make him happier?" "What does he want me to know?" and "Does he know how much I love him?" The behavior questions are still asked, as are health questions, but the change in the owners' attitudes toward their pets is overwhelming. I have seen a move from a throw-away society where animals are routinely euthanized in humane societies to no-kill shelters and rescue facilities. In these new facilities animals of all types and sizes can be rehabilitated mentally and physically and be adopted; or, if they cannot be rehabilitated, they live the remainder of their lives being well cared for in a safe, secure environment.

I like to feel that, as humans, our spiritual levels of awareness about who we are, why we are on this planet and why the animals are here with us reflect a positive side of our human growth and evolution. Of course, it can be said that my spiritual growth has put me in touch with more people whose thoughts are similar to my own. This is partially correct but I have seen too many changes in my clients and in the animals I meet to believe that this is the whole reason.

Another often-asked question is, "why is this animal in my life and what am I to learn from him or her?" People are becoming aware that their pets can act as filters for their owners' emotional or physical problems. I have clients whose pets have developed cancer after their owner was diagnosed with the same disease. Other clients have pets who reflect the owner's weakened immune system. In my opinion this is a way our pets show their love and concern for us. Animals may develop an illness similar to their owner's illness, in an effort to help the owner heal his or her human body. This ability to reflect emotional issues, or to develop a similar illness to its owner's, has shown me that this is the animal's way of trying to remove emotional or physical problems from the owner.

Owners who ask me what they can learn from their pets usually expect to hear the answers "unconditional love" or "patience." However, by watching our animal friends enjoy life we can also learn to live in the moment and enjoy each experience that comes into our lives.

One final question that I hear frequently concerns the issue of reincarnation. I read for many owners who have felt a strong or familiar connection with a new pet or animal that entered their life. The animals are very willing to confirm a place in past lives with their current owner. The connection may have occurred many lives ago, or your childhood companion may have returned to accompany you in later years of your life. I know from working with clients and their pets that our animals can make a quick transition, returning in a year or less to reconnect with a much loved owner for another visit on this plane. We have to remember that the animals have free will, just as we do, and that a quick return can happen.

As we move into what I see as a more enlightened and spiritual phase for the earth, I believe more people will become aware of what we can learn from the animals and how they can raise our levels of spiritual awareness. It is my hope in teaching animal communication that more people will become aware of how interrelated we are with the earth and see the unlimited experiences that are available to us when we make a connection with the animals and other nonverbal spirits who share this planet with us.

Maybelle, one of my adopted donkeys

Joe Dog, guarding the yard.

Sunshine, no longer a wild dog

Tessie Catahoula was the first dog to visit me from spirit

Virginianna, our farm in Paris, Kentucky

Tom with Lullabelle after her adoption

The Black Swans patrolling the lake

My first crossbred geese were first in line for corn

Tony Llama helps himself to dinner

Hildy on the alert

Bold Paddy in retirement

Briar Patch, my first Paint horse

Bold Paddy and the author compete at the
Pennsylvania National Horse Show

Our strong connection turned horse shows into a joy

for Bold Paddy and me

The author with her husband, Tom

Judy Fuson

My childhood home in Lexington, Kentucky

Mollie contemplating her past lives

Berrie, no longer a rambunctious puppy

Morgan balances on one of her high perches

Sunshine, on left, and Joe, on right, enjoy a game of tag

"Where's the herd?" Lilly Llama surveys the farm

Charlie, in the Winner's Circle at Keeneland Race Track

Watchkitty, left and R.T. right compete for the author's lap

Smokey, one of my early animal guides

Frazier, the ex-racer, decided he was a farm dog at heart

Blackberry, who will always be one of my most memorable dogs

GLOSSARY

ANGELS—Very evolved spiritual beings who are with us to offer protection and guidance. Angels have not lived in a human body but have evolved in the spirit realms. I feel they give us joy, protection and guidance. I also believe that they can take on a physical or other life form to help us during our journey on earth.

ANIMALS IN SPIRIT—When animals die they go through a physical transformation. This change results in the soul or spirit leaving the physical body that housed the spirit while it was on earth. The energy that is the soul or spirit simply changes to a new shape and form. The essential spirit remains the same and moves on to a spiritual realm. The transformation at death is the same for animals and humans.

PASSING OR GOING INTO SPIRIT—This is a time of transformation. All humans and animals leave the earth plane and return to the spiritual plane. They no longer need the dense body used on earth, the soul or ethereal body returns home to the spiritual plane. There is no death but simply a transformation of the energetic shape and form. On the spiritual plane we reconnect with the powerful Universal Energy that created us.

PAST LIVES AND REINCARNATION—The belief that humans and animals have experienced many different lives on earth. Each soul, human or animal, returns to a new body. The return trips enable the spirit to work on different lessons during its spiritual journey. We take on these spiritual journeys that eventually lead us to the fulfillment of our soul growth. I believe humans return to work on their own life lessons, while animals return to help humans and experience lessons that further the person's spiritual growth. Animals also reincarnate to reconnect with human companions or to simply experience life on a different plane.

PAST LIFE REGRESSIONS—Regressions are a mental journey into other life times that we have led on earth. This information may come to us while we meditate or during hypnosis. Our past life information is stored in our subconscious. We can access the information by working with our spirit guides or with people trained to help us uncover this information.

SPIRIT GUIDES—These are highly evolved beings that help and direct us in our spiritual journey. They have lived on earth and experienced life in a physical body. All of us have spirit guides who protect us and give us information. Working with us on the spiritual plane also helps the guides grow and progress on their own spiritual journey. They will cycle in and out of our lives and new guides will enter to help us as we grow spiritually. Guides can be animals that we have known or they can be family or friends who have chosen to work with us from the spiritual plane.

UNIVERSAL ENERGY—The God or Creator energy that exists all around us. The force that creates all living things.

Judy Fuson

ABOUT THE AUTHOR

The author grew up on her parents' Thoroughbred horse farm in Lexington, Kentucky. Her lifelong love of horses led to a career as a trainer of show horses and riding instructor. When she inherited her family's horse business her work with horses moved from the show ring to full time management of a breeding farm.

She was introduced to the world of animal communication after meeting Beatrice Lydecker, an animal communicator from California. Nonverbal communication became a large part of her work with horses and eventually led to consultations with dogs, cats, birds and a variety of other pets.

In 1997 she sold her farm and now travels doing consultations for pets and their caretakers as well as lectures and workshops where she teaches animal communication. The author believes that talking with animals is a skill that anyone can learn. This book gives insight into the thoughts of all animals and outlines her method of teaching people to talk with their pets.

Judy lives in Tucson, Arizona with her family: Berrie, a Scottish Terrier and Mollie, a Manx cat. She is currently finishing her second book on animal thoughts and communication.

LaVergne, TN USA
28 August 2009

156353LV00002B/81/A